Trade Policy Review

Ghana

1992

General Agreement on Tariffs and Trade
Geneva, May 1992
Volume II

V O L U M E   II

TABLE OF CONTENTS

Volume I contains the report by the GATT Secretariat.

PREFACE

As one of the mid-term results of the Uruguay Round, the CONTRACTING PARTIES established the Trade Policy Review Mechanism (TPRM), on a trial basis, in April 1989.

The objectives of the TPRM are to contribute to improved adherence by all contracting parties to GATT rules, disciplines and commitments, and hence to the smoother functioning of the multilateral trading system, by achieving greater transparency in, and understanding of, the trade policies and practices of contracting parties. Accordingly, the review mechanism enables the regular collective appreciation and evaluation by the CONTRACTING PARTIES of the full range of individual contracting parties' trade policies and practices and their impact on the functioning of the multilateral trading system. It is not, however, intended to serve as a basis for the enforcement of specific GATT obligations or for dispute settlement procedures, or to impose new policy commitments on contracting parties.

The assessment to be carried out under the review mechanism takes place, to the extent relevant, against the background of the wider economic and developmental needs, policies and objectives of the contracting party concerned, as well of its external environment. However, the function of the review mechanism is to examine the impact of a contracting party's trade policies and practices on the multilateral trading system.

Under the TPRM, the trade policies of all contracting parties are subject to periodic review. The four largest trading entities in terms of world market share, counting the European Communities as one, are reviewed every two years, the next largest 16 trading entities every four years, and other contracting parties every six years, except that a longer period may be fixed for least-developed countries.

The reviews are conducted by the GATT Council, in special meetings, on the basis of two reports, one presented by the contracting party under review and another drawn up by the GATT Secretariat on its own responsibility. Following each review, the reports, together with the minutes of the Council meeting, are published.

The present volumes cover the review of Ghana conducted by the Council on 9-10 March 1992 under the Chairmanship of Mr. B.K. Zutshi.

P A R T   A

CONCLUDING REMARKS BY THE CHAIRMAN

OF THE COUNCIL

AMBASSADOR ZUTSHI

IN THE COUNCIL MEETING ON THE

TRADE POLICY REVIEW OF GHANA

9-10 MARCH 1992

This special meeting of the Council has collectively reviewed and evaluated Ghana's trade policies and practices, including their impact on the functioning of the multilateral trading system. The statements made during the meeting by the Ghanaian delegation and other participants will be reflected in the minutes. These remarks are intended to summarize, on my own responsibility, the salient points emerging from this review.

The representative of Ghana opened the discussion by outlining the basic objectives of the ongoing programme of trade and economic reforms followed by Ghana since 1983 under the Economic Recovery Programme. An essential ingredient of these reforms had been to improve the country's resource allocation as well as its productive and export capacities, through greater reliance on market forces and an increasing role for the private sector, while maintaining responsible monetary and fiscal policies. Public sector efforts focused on effective implementation of policy reforms and improving the physical and social infrastructure.

Efforts taken to liberalize the trading regime in Ghana included the removal of import licensing and tariff reductions, together with the introduction of a market-determined exchange rate. Further steps announced in the 1992 Budget included abolition of the super sales tax; rationalization of the special additional import tax rates, formerly of between 10 and 40 per cent, to a maximum rate of 10 per cent; the scaling down of import and sales taxes on motor cars and abolition of duties on building materials as well as, inter alia, reductions in company tax rates in commerce and other service areas. As Ghana's economy became more outward looking, however, its need for better access to foreign markets and a stronger international trading system would be more critical.

Participants recognized that Ghana, as a low-income developing country with a natural resource-based economy, a limited export base and a high level of indebtedness, had faced many serious constraints in a responsible manner. Its impressive achievements to date in economic reform, with trade and exchange liberalization at the centre, had strengthened its integration in the world economy and improved its economic performance.

Ghana had ceased to use trade restrictions for balance-of-payments purposes, had reduced tariffs and thus exposed its economy to greater international competition. The Council commended Ghana for the way that, with the aid of substantial external assistance, it had resolutely tackled the challenges before it using comprehensive economic reforms. The important role played by autonomous trade liberalization in redressing the inefficiencies caused by past import-substitution policies was emphasized.

One participant suggested that trade liberalization by itself was unlikely to fully solve Ghana's economic problems and that export incentives were a legitimate trade policy instrument for diversifying exports of processed products, provided they did not impose excessive costs elsewhere in the economy.

Participants raised questions and sought further information from Ghana on a variety of issues, including:

- the effects on trade and production incentives of Ghana's escalating tariff structure and various tax concessions;

- the use of minimum import prices and special import tariffs, including for anti-dumping purposes;

- the role of the recently established Tax Tribunal in customs matters;

- Ghana's experience in the field of export diversification and the use of export incentives, such as income tax rebates;

- the use and potential effects on resource allocation of export restrictions on unprocessed products, especially timber, to promote domestic value-added in the sector;

- Ghana's aims and policies in the area of agricultural development;

- Ghana's ongoing privatization programme;

- policies relating to foreign investment;

- the revised basic trade law under consideration in Ghana;

- details regarding Ghana's proposed new patent legislation; and

- Ghana's experience as a member of ECOWAS and its views on the functioning of that organization, and the proposed creation of the African Economic Community.

It was noted that Ghana had bound none of its tariffs in GATT. Participants also asked whether Ghana would join any of the MTN Agreements.

In responding to these questions and comments, the representative of Ghana reiterated his Government's commitment to further trade reforms, including the gradual lowering of tariffs to more uniform levels, and reductions in the scope for duty exemptions and concessions. A major aspect of its policy thrust was to reduce the economy's vulnerability to world commodity price movements through export diversification away from traditional exports, such as cocoa, towards non-traditional manufactured and primary exports, including fish, salt, processed food, soaps, wood and aluminium products. The activities of the Export Promotion Council were important in this regard. The stimulation of greater private sector involvement was also receiving high priority, through acceleration of the divestiture programme and other policies, such as tax concessions and financial reforms. He emphasized that the Government's role was one of providing the infrastructural facilities necessary for economic growth.

Details were given on the important role played by overseas remittances, as well as external assistance, in supporting the balance of payments and the reform programme. The impending establishment of the Tax Tribunal, with High Court status, would be an important advance in customs administration. Ghana would give consideration to binding its tariffs, but thought that further tariff reforms should precede any binding commitments. The reduction of the Government's role in marketing of primary products would be continued. Steps would soon be taken to remove COCOBOD's monopoly position on domestic cocoa sales, although it was thought necessary to maintain its sole export responsibilities for quality control purposes, among others. Ghana was considering acceding to MTN Agreements, especially those on Technical Barriers to Trade, Customs Valuation, Government Procurement and Import Licensing. However, this would be heavily influenced by the outcome of the Uruguay Round. There had been a renewed interest in regional trade initiatives, such as ECOWAS and the proposed African Economic Community, following the strengthening of international trade blocs elsewhere in the world. Other matters raised by participants would be covered in a written response.

Members agreed with the representative of Ghana on the importance to its reform programme of a successful outcome to the Uruguay Round, especially in tropical products, natural resource-based products and agriculture. Improved market access in these areas would significantly assist Ghana achieving its full export potential, and help further reduce its dependence on cocoa. At the same time, Ghana could make its contribution to the Round and increase the stability and predictability of its own trade policies through tariff bindings.

The Council commended Ghana for the substantial progress that it had made in economic liberalization, in the face of considerable difficulties. The implementation of further reforms, including continuing reductions in tariffs and greater divestiture of State-owned enterprises, would strengthen Ghana's economic potential. However, Ghana's autonomous liberalization efforts must be matched by its trading partners, within the multilateral system, by ensuring favourable market access and stable trading conditions for its export growth and diversification.

P A R T   B

REPORT BY THE GOVERNMENT OF GHANA

CONTENTS

TRADE POLICY REVIEW MECHANISM

GHANA

EXECUTIVE SUMMARY

Ghana, with an estimated population of 15 million is a sub-Saharan African country with an open economy which depends on a few primary commodity exports of mainly cocoa, timber and minerals. About 70 per cent of the population live in rural areas where they depend directly or indirectly on agricultural and related activities for their livelihood.

At the time of independence in 1957, Ghana operated a liberal import régime which was supported by commodity exports of which cocoa, timber and minerals contributed over 95 per cent of export earnings. With the accelerated development programme placing a high premium on industrialization, the manufacturing sector grew rapidly, increasing its share of GDP from 2 per cent in 1957 to 9 per cent in 1969. This brought heavy pressure on foreign exchange earnings by way of raw material imports together with machinery and equipment. As the disequilibrium in external payments deepened various measures were introduced to restrict imports. These included exchange controls, import licensing, quantitative restrictions and high tariffs.

Attempts were also made in the late 1960s to revamp the export sector through export diversification by setting up the Ghana Export Promotion Council (GEPC) and the Ghana Export Company (GEC). The GEPC was to develop and promote exports, while the GEC was to undertake the physical export of non-traditional products. Exporters were also provided with a number of incentives. Further trade measures introduced in the seventies to combat the balance-of-payments problem included the setting up of a State agency - the Ghana National Procurement Agency (GNPA) to undertake the bulk purchase of specified essential commodities. Countertrade measures which had been initiated with East European countries in the sixties were reinforced and expanded as a means of increasing exports and saving foreign exchange for priority imports. Economic relations established within the framework of Permanent Joint Commissions for Co-operation were also used as a vehicle for expanding non-traditional exports into other African countries.

Thus by 1981 an institutional framework and various measures and incentives had been established in the attempt to address the balance-of-payments problem. In spite of all these measures, the balance-of-payments situation rather worsened. Rapid inflation, low savings and low investment as well as unrealistic exchange rates, led to disincentives for export production, higher propensity to import, acute foreign exchange shortage and therefore general social and economic decline. It was against this background that the Economic Recovery Programme (ERP) was launched in 1983.

Priority objectives of the ERP in the trade sector have focused on the establishment of a buoyant and self-sustaining export sector, efficient and effective import management, as well as the development of a vibrant tourism sector. To this effect, measures that have been adopted include the rehabilitation of the traditional export sector and the development and expansion of non-traditional products; export diversification; adoption of a market-determined exchange rate system; trade liberalization, including removal of licensing and price controls. Other measures are tariff and tax reforms; utilization of foreign exchange earnings in the most efficient and cost effective manner; rehabilitation of port and communications facilities; and tourism infrastructural development.

Even though these measures have led to some modest improvement in the performance of the export sector, the issue of narrow export base still remains. There has therefore been a renewed effort at export development, promotion and diversification. While the market improvement in the economy will certainly enhance the success of this effort, a more liberalized and open multilateral trading system within the framework of an invigorated GATT will no doubt contribute a great deal to the attainment of Ghana's objectives. It is for this reason that Ghana is actively participating in the Uruguay Round and committed to its successful conclusion.

A.   TRADE POLICIES AND PRACTICES

(i)   Objectives of trade policies

The Economic Recovery Programme (ERP) which was launched in 1983 aimed essentially at removing market distortions which prevented the price mechanism from allocating resources effectively. It also sought to re-organise the country's productive structure through price incentives. The ERP pursued various monetary, fiscal, incomes and exchange rate policies to achieve its set objectives. These measures and the various incentives have benefited the trade sector of the economy.

Following the adoption of the ERP and the various Structural Adjustment Programmes (SAPs) under it, trade policy has been directed towards the following general objectives:

-      Restoring incentives for the production of food, industrial raw materials and export commodities, and thereby increasing their output to realistic levels;

-      Increasing the availability of essential consumer goods, machinery and equipment and improving the distribution system; and

-      Increasing the overall availability of foreign exchange, improving its allocation mechanism, and channelling it into selected high priority activities.

In line with these objectives, production in the agricultural minerals and wood sectors have been stepped up to increase export earnings. Export diversification and further processing are being encouraged to expand the country's export base and move away from the mono-crop dependence on cocoa which still accounts for almost 41 per cent of Ghana's exports.

In order to allow the market mechanism to determine the allocation of resources, most quantitative and qualitative restrictions have been removed. Price controls have been eliminated, and restrictions on payments and transfers with regard to international transactions have also been eased.

By and large, therefore, Ghana's trade policy is beginning to reflect a strong belief in international competitiveness, and the recognition that protectionism and import controls can only prevent the levels of economic growth associated internationally with competition-induced structural change. This policy outlook has been reflected in the deregulation of the exchange rate mechanism, the dismantling of the import licensing system, the gradual lowering of general tariff levels, the removal of support for and the privatization of State-owned enterprises.

Sectoral trade policies

(a) Agriculture

In recognition of the leading rôle of agriculture in the national economy, programmes are generally aimed at evolving development-oriented, productivity-enhancing and competitiveness-promoting agricultural practices. Policies are therefore geared towards the following broad objectives:

- to ensure adequate and sustainable production of food and industrial raw materials;

- to make Ghana's agriculture competitive on the world market;

- to expand and diversify agricultural production as a way of strengthening the foreign exchange earning capability to help improve the balance-of-payments position; and

- to increase incentives to farmers and thus improve the quality of life and the environment.

As regards pricing policy, producer prices have been reviewed periodically to maintain the incentive element. Subsidies on fertiliser have been removed, while fertiliser marketing is being privatized in phases. Tariffs on agricultural inputs generally carry very low duty rates.

(b) Industry

In line with the ERP, current industrial policies are aimed at creating the enabling environment which encourages private participation in industries based on the use of local raw material resources. The objectives of Ghana's industrial policy are to strengthen functional linkages with agriculture and natural resources, to increase the development and exploitation of natural resources, and to re-orient enterprises and industry towards efficiency, competitiveness, higher productivity and self-sustaining growth. Incentive schemes are provided under the Investment Code to encourage industries to locate outside urban centres, and to produce for export.

(c) Forestry

The general objectives of policies for the development of the forestry sector are:

-    the proper management of forest resources; and

-    increasing revenue, especially foreign exchange.

Efforts are being directed towards increasing domestic value-added in the processing of timber products, and the development of an integrated wood-working sector, as well as bringing on-stream more furniture and joinery units aimed at producing quality products for the export market. Measures have also been designed to promote forestry conservation, including re-planting and agro-forestry development as well as minimising the reckless dissipation of the forest base.

(ii)   Description of the import and export system

(a) Imports

In line with the ERP the various import control measures have been dismantled. With the removal of import licensing, importers are only required to complete an import declaration form, which serves mainly for import monitoring and statistical purposes. All imports valued at US$5,000 and above are subject to pre-shipment inspection.

A few products require special permits for their importation, for reasons of health, public morality, plant life and security.

State organizations are used for bulk importation of some consumer items. These however do not constitute monopoly positions but are aimed at ensuring that imports are available at competitive prices.

(b) Exports

Priority objectives under the ERP in the trade sector have focused on the development of a buoyant and self-sustaining export sector. Efforts have, therefore, been directed towards maximising returns. The export licensing system has been abolished and export procedures and documentation have been streamlined. Exporters of non-traditional products are required to obtain the Exchange Control Form A2 issued by the Bank of Ghana or the authorised dealer-banks. Export incentives are under regular review to ensure their effectiveness. The exportation of some traditional products are carried out by designated State organizations as follows:

(1) The Cocoa Marketing Company, a subsidiary of Ghana Cocoa Board is responsible for the sale and exportation of cocoa beans, cocoa products, coffee and sheanuts. Sales are by private treaty on the basis of world market values at the best prices obtainable, and negotiations are governed by normal commercial considerations.

(2) Timber Export Development Board (TEDB) is to develop markets for lesser known timber species and to promote the sale and export of Ghana's timber products. The Board does not engage in export directly.

(3) Precious Minerals Marketing Corporation is charged with securing the most favourable arrangements for the purchase, grading, valuing, export and sale of diamond and gold produced or processed in Ghana won by small-scale operators. However, large mining companies export on their own under valid licences granted by the Ministry of Lands and Natural Resources. There are no export levies on the export of processed or unprocessed minerals. Companies are permitted to negotiate their own sales and marketing agreements which are subject to approval from the Minerals Commission and the Bank of Ghana.

In special cases, applications for export (approved A2 Form) should be supported by permits from appropriate organizations as indicated below:

(a) Live animals and pets: a valid health certificate from the Department of Animal Health and Productivity.

(b) Wild animals: a valid permit from the Department of Game and Wildlife.

(c) Antiques and handicrafts: a valid permit issued by The Museum and Monuments Board.

(d) Scrap metals (non-ferrous): a police inspection report.

(e) Firearms: a police permit.

(f) Plants and seeds: should be supported by a permit from the Plant and Quarantine Department of the Ministry of Agriculture.

(g) Timber (round and sawn): with the exception of major exporters registered by the Bureau, all else should have a permit issued by the Forest Products Inspection Bureau.

Efforts are, however, being pursued to centralise the issuing of these special export permits.

(iii)   The Trade policy framework

(a) Domestic laws and regulations governing the application of trade
     policies

     The principal law regulating trade is the Imports and Exports Act 418
of 1980, which has been rendered obsolete in the light of the current trade
liberalization measures. A more comprehensive basic trade law is therefore
under consideration. Other laws, regulations and decrees governing trade
policies are:

     -   Exchange Control Act, 1960 (Act 71)

     This law is being reviewed to bring it into line with the current
exchange deregulation practices.

     -   Customs and Excise Decree 1972 and the Customs Regulations 1976
         (L.I. 1060)

     These Laws provide for:

     (a) Customs and excise tariffs;

     (b) Payment of duty, refunds, drawbacks;

     (c) Goods used contrary to an authorised purpose; and

     (d) Exemption from payment of customs duties.

The same Legislative Instrument L.I.1060 makes provisions for regulations
on customs valuation.

     -   Imports and Exports (Special Licence) Regulations, 1985
         (L.I.1314)

     This regulates the importation of cigarettes, stout beer, asbestos
(roofing sheets) and fibre cement pipes.

     -   Pharmacy and Drugs Act, 1961 (Act 64)

     Among other things this empowers the Minister/Secretary for Health to
grant licences for the importation of dangerous drugs.

     -   Arms and Ammunition Regulations, 1972 (NLCD 9)

     Requires importers of arms and ammunition to obtain a licence before
placing orders.

- <u>Mercury Law (PNDC Law 217), 1985</u>

Requires importers of mercury to obtain a licence from the Ministry of Trade and Tourism for safety, public health and security reasons.

- <u>The Prevention and Control of Pests and Diseases of Plants Act</u>
  <u>(Act 307)</u>

This Act is designed to protect plants from being infested with foreign diseases and pests.

- <u>Ghana National Trading Corporation (GNTC) Law (L.I.1395)</u>

Establishes GNTC as a State-trading organization.

- <u>Procurement Agency Decree, 1976</u>

Establishes GNPA as a State-procurement organization.

- <u>Ghana Supply Commission Law (PNDC Law 245)</u>

Sets up the GSC as the sole procurement agency for all government supplies and stores.

- <u>The Ghana Investments Code, 1985 (PNDC Law 116)</u>

Regulates investments in the Ghanaian economy.

- <u>Imports and Exports (Non-Traditional Exports) Regulations</u>
  <u>(L.I. 1354)</u>

Deals with the export of non-traditional products.

- <u>National Museum Regulations, 1973 (E.I.29)</u>

Regulates the exports of antiques.

- <u>Cocoa Board Law (PNDC Law 81)</u>

Vests Cocobod with the sole authority to undertake among other things, the export and processing of cocoa, coffee and sheanuts.

- <u>Standards Board Decree (NRCD 173)</u>

This established the National Standards Board. Among its functions the NSB is to advise the Minister responsible for Trade on the standard requirements for importation into Ghana.

- <u>Ghana Standards (Food, Drugs and other Goods)</u>
  <u>General Labelling Rules, 1991 (L.I.1512)</u>

Provides that any food or drug and other goods being imported into Ghana should be clearly marked and labelled.

- <u>Minerals and Mining Law, 1984 (PNDC Law 153)</u>

This Law vests all minerals in the PNDC which holds them in trust for the people of Ghana. Under Section 3(1) of the Law, no person shall export, sell or otherwise dispose of any mineral unless he holds a licence granted by the Secretary for Lands and Natural Resources for that purpose.

- <u>Trade Fairs Authority Law, 1989 (PNDC Law 215)</u>

This Law established the Ghana Trade Fair Authority with the principal aim of planning, promotion and organization of trade fairs, exhibitions and other commercial activities or shows in Ghana or to represent Ghana in any such exhibitions or fairs abroad.

(b) <u>Summary description of the process of trade policy formulation and review, as well as responsibilities and institutional functioning of bodies primarily involved in this process and with the administration of trade policies</u>

Trade policy formulation and review in Ghana is the responsibility of the Government of Ghana. In the absence of a parliament this responsibility is vested primarily in the Ministry of Trade and Tourism. In the exercise of this responsibility the Secretary for Trade and Tourism consults with various relevant Ministries, departments and bodies both private and public, which provide inputs. The draft policy that ensues from such consultations is presented for consideration to the Committee of Secretaries which in turn sends it to the Provisional National Defence Council for final approval.

The main bodies involved are, therefore, the following:

- <u>Ministry of Trade and Tourism</u>

The Ministry has overall responsibility for trade matters and it initiates policies and organises activities for the development and promotion of trade.

- <u>Bank of Ghana</u>

The Bank of Ghana has responsibility for implementing the Government's exchange rate and monetary policies as well as making balance-of-payments forecasts.

- ### Customs, Excise and Preventive Service (CEPS)

Statutorily, in addition to its excise functions, the CEPS is responsible for border protection and administration of Ghana's customs and tariff régime.

- ### Ministry of Finance and Economic Planning

This Ministry has overall responsibility for the formulation and review of the country's monetary, fiscal and exchange rate policies and, therefore, overseas the operations of the Bank of Ghana, CEPS and the Internal Revenue Service.

- ### Ministry of Agriculture

The Ministry initiates some trade-related agricultural policies and its views are sought on policy matters relating to trade in certain agricultural products, particularly food, fish and fish products, plant and importation of pesticides.

- ### Ministry of Lands and Natural Resources

It is under the aegis of this Ministry that the Timber Export Development Board and the Minerals Commission respectively promote the sale and export of Ghana's timber products and minerals other than gold.

- ### Ministry of Health

The Ministry is responsible for the importation of drugs and pharmaceutical products. It is also responsible for the implementation of health regulations and sanitary laws to ensure that wholesome food items are exchanged across the frontiers of Ghana for human consumption.

- ### The Ghana Export Promotion Council (GEPC)

Under the aegis of the Ministry of Trade and Tourism the GEPC has been charged with the responsibility of developing and promoting the exports of Ghana's non-traditional products.

- ### The Ghana Standards Board

This is a statutory body which ensures that imports and exports are in conformity with standards acceptable by international organizations to which Ghana is a member, such as the CODEX Alimentarius Commission, the International Organization for Standardization and the International Electrotechnical Commission.

- **The Ghana National Chamber of Commerce**

The Chamber, which has regional branches, offers inputs for trade policy formulation and review after consultation with its members.

- **Association of Ghana Industries (AGI)**

The AGI also provides inputs on policy matters relating to the promotion, sale and export of manufactures as well as matters relating to incentives for the manufacturing sector.

- **Private individuals**

Besides the public and private bodies, the Ministry of Trade and Tourism seeks the views of individuals who are considered to have expertise and experience in trade and trade-related matters.

(c) **Multilateral, bilateral and regional trading arrangements, their scope, duration and goals**

Ghana participates in a number of trading arrangements with the objectives of ensuring friendly bilateral relations and an orderly multilateral trading system, diversifying her trading links, expanding her export markets and promoting south-south trade.

(1) **MULTILATERAL AGREEMENTS**

(a) **General Agreement on Tariffs and Trade (GATT)**

Ghana acceded to the GATT in 1957, and has since participated in previous multilateral trade negotiations under the auspices of the GATT, including the Tokyo Round. With the hope that a strengthened GATT system will go a long way to improving her trade performance, Ghana is actively participating in and committed to a successful completion of the Uruguay Round.

(b) **United Nations Conference on Trade and Development (UNCTAD)**

Ghana is a member of UNCTAD and an active participant in the work of its various committees. Ghana is also a member of the World Bank and the International Monetary Fund.

(c) **The Lomé Convention**

Ghana is a signatory to the ACP-EEC (Lomé) Convention. This is a Treaty on trade and economic co-operation between the EEC and sixty-eight African, Caribbean and Pacific countries under which the products of these countries have preferential access to EEC markets.

(2) REGIONAL AGREEMENTS

Ghana is a founding member of the Economic Community of West African States (ECOWAS) which was formed in 1975. The aim is to facilitate the free flow of goods and services among member countries, leading ultimately to a free-trade area and a common customs union.

(3) BILATERAL AGREEMENTS

Ghana has concluded bilateral trade and payments agreements with a number of African countries and centrally-planned economies. With the dismantling of central planning and the introduction of market economies in Eastern Europe the agreements with USSR, Hungary, Poland, Romania and Yugoslavia are being reviewed with the aim of bringing them into line with open-market practices. In the case of the former GDR, a German company has taken over the trading arrangements and reverted to the normal market-economy system. The agreement with China is also being reviewed to operate on a cash basis, while that of Cuba has been reviewed for another two years.

As regards African countries, bilateral agreements exist with Libya, Burkina Faso, Mauritania, Nigeria and Zimbabwe. These agreements do not entail any special tariff concessions, but only provide a framework for trade exchanges within the context of intra-African trade co-operation.

(iv)   The implementation of trade policies

(a) Trade policy measures used by the contracting party, their implementation during the period under review, including developments in different sectors, and comparison with their use in earlier periods

Ghana's trade policy measures currently in place include the following:

-     Tariffs

Since the introduction of the ERP, Ghana's tariff structure has been reviewed and adjusted to the extent that it now provides for a relatively uniform and moderate level of protection, with most duty rates ranging from 0 to 25 per cent.

In general, import duties are levied on an ad valorem basis. The Government intends to further restructure tariffs with a view to making them more responsive to economic development, and creating a lower and more uniform pattern of protection. This process will involve lower standard rates, a reduction in the scope of duty exemptions and concessions as well as streamlining of the duty drawback scheme to improve its effectiveness.

All imports enter Ghana at m.f.n. rates except for a few imports that receive preferential tariff treatment under ECOWAS trading arrangements.

-   Levies and other charges

Super sales taxes, introduced in 1990, are levied on some categories of imported luxury goods. The initial rates, which ranged from 75-500 per cent, now fall between 30-100 per cent. Luxury goods so defined are currently not produced domestically, and the rates are therefore not protective.

-   Preferential trading arrangement

Ghana is a member of the sixteen-nation Economic Community of West African States (ECOWAS). Even though a trade co-operation arrangement provides for a phase-out of tariffs leading to a customs union, implementation has fallen well behind schedule.

-   Customs valuation

The calculation of the dutiable value of imported goods is done by the customs and excise authorities. Tariffs are levied on the normal c.i.f. price of the product in accordance with the Brussels Definition of Value (BDV). Ghana is, however, considering the adoption of the GATT Customs Valuation Code.

-   Rules of origin

A rule of origin legislation is currently being considered under the basic trade law under preparation. Currently, Ghana operates only the ECOWAS rules of origin.

-   Tax rebates

In 1991 corporate tax rebates were increased from a minimum range of 30-40 per cent to a maximum range of 60-75 per cent. The schedule is as follows:

Sector	Product exported	Before 1991	1991
Agriculture	5% - 15%	30%	40%
	16% - 25%	50%	60%
	above 25%	60%	75%
Manufacturing	5% - 15%	25%	30%
	16% - 25%	30%	50%
	above 25%	60%	75%

The beneficiaries are primarily those who engage in agricultural production or manufacturing for export.

- Tariff exemptions and concessionary duty rates

Tariff exemptions are granted to Government, privileged persons and certain organizations and institutions. These include diplomatic missions, UN agencies, the British Council, technical assistance schemes and items for trade fairs and exhibitions.

A number of intermediate goods are also admissible at concessionary duty rates when imported by manufacturers. These include unmanufactured tobacco, raw materials including packing materials for pharmaceutical products, plastic granules imported by Cocobod and materials of base metal for the production of agricultural implements.

- Government procurement

(i)   The Ghana Supply Commission (GSC)

The GSC derives its authority as the principal procurement agency for Government from Act 7 of 1960. This has been replaced by the Ghana Supply Commission Law, 1990, PNDC Law 245.

The Commission's purchasing policy is based on world-wide competitive tendering practices except where negotiation at Government level is considered appropriate.

Purchases and contracts exceeding US$99,000 (ninety nine thousand US dollars) in value are advertised. Competitive tenders usually have global circulation. There are no regional references currently in force.

(ii)   The Ghana National Procurement Agency (GNPA)

The GNPA is a centralized purchasing organization that has been charged with the responsibility of purchasing in bulk both within and outside Ghana, certain commodities that are designated as essential commodities by the Secretary for Trade and Tourism. This organization is not the sole importer of these products which are also open to all other importing agencies.

The Agency follows three systems of purchasing, i.e. the international competitive bidding or the open tender system, as well as government-to-government negotiations.

- **State-trading enterprises**

(i)   **Ghana National Trading Corporation (GNTC)**

The GNTC was established in 1961 by Executive Instrument No. 203 as a State-trading enterprise. GNTC is expected to compete and operate like any other commercial (private) house, and does not enjoy any special facilities from government.

(ii)   **Ghana Food Distribution Corporation (GFDC)**

GFDC was established under Legislative Instrument 714 in November 1971. Its objective is to purchase, store, preserve, sell and distribute foodstuffs including meat, fish, and fish and meat preparations. Under the Legislative Instrument 714, the Corporation is charged to conduct its affairs on sound commercial lines.

- **Foreign exchange arrangements and restrictions**

In February 1988, the Government authorised the establishment of forex bureaux by individuals, companies and banks for the purchase and sale of foreign exchange as part of the liberalization of the trade and exchange system.

All _bona fide_ requests for foreign exchange for imports and other payments are funded through the weekly auction system. Currently dealer banks and forex bureaux are permitted, under the wholesale auction, to purchase foreign exchange from the Bank of Ghana, and the exchange rate is determined using the Dutch marginal pricing system.

- **Countertrade**

Countertrade arrangements have been used in Ghana's trade relations since the 1960's with the erstwhile centrally-planned economies of Eastern Europe, Asia and other developing countries. Under these agreements Ghana exchanged cocoa, copra, manganese, rough diamonds, tropical wood and wood products for sugar, pharmaceuticals, transport equipment, construction projects and consumer goods. The main countries were China, Cuba, Poland, USSR, GDR, Romania, India, Yugoslavia and Hungary.

With the adoption of open-market practices in the socialist countries, the countertrade agreements are being replaced with open market-based arrangements.

(b) <u>Programmes in existence for trade liberalization, including those agreed in the context of structural adjustment and/or debt negotiations</u>

In Ghana, trade liberalization was preceded by a stabilization package and a series of currency devaluations. This was followed by a move towards exchange-rate liberalization through the two-tier window system which was later merged. The fixed rate window was essential to reduce the impact of the exchange-rate liberalization on Government expenditures.

A weekly exchange rate auction was introduced in September 1986. In February 1988, the buying and selling of foreign exchange was legalised, and forex bureaux were set up. The only information requirement on the bureaux were that they should clearly display the rates, and report sales/purchases to the Bank of Ghana on a monthly basis.

Concurrent with the evolution of the exchange and payment régime towards a market-based system was a gradual relaxation of import and export controls. In February 1989, the whole import licensing system was abolished, and importers were required only to file an import declaration form at the commercial banks and/or at entry points.

On the export side, the requirement to obtain an export licence was removed and export documentations simplified. The retention scheme was improved, and the exporters of non-traditional exports were allowed to sell the balances in their retention accounts on the bureaux markets.

(c) <u>Prospective changes in trade policies and practices to the extent that these changes are already announced or can be made known</u>

Necessary legislation has been passed to establish an independent tax tribunal for hearing appeals against customs decisions and tax related complaints.

The Government is also considering the introduction of an export credit guarantee Scheme to help exporters obtain loans which are currently difficult to obtain from the main banking system, and there are proposals to discontinue exports of cocoa under countertrade and bilateral trade and payment arrangements.

The Government is committed to further reducing the standard import duty rates; transferring the rôle of luxury taxation to excise and sales taxes; phasing-out special import taxes; and establishing procedures for reviewing rates of duty on particular products.

The government is also committed to providing further incentives for export production by improving exporters' access to working capital.

The establishment of export processing zones is receiving the attention of Government.

B. RELEVANT BACKGROUND AGAINST WHICH THE ASSESSMENT OF TRADE POLICIES WILL BE CARRIED OUT: WIDER ECONOMIC AND DEVELOPMENTAL NEEDS, EXTERNAL ENVIRONMENT

(i)   Wider economic and developmental needs, policies and objectives

As indicated in A(i), with the support of the Fund and the World Bank and increasing assistance from the donor community, Ghana has since 1983 embarked upon an Economic Recovery Programme (ERP) in an attempt to reverse the declining trends in the economy and achieve a sustainable rate of economic growth and equilibrium in external payments.

The broad objectives of the programme were:

(a) to design incentive schemes in favour of the productive base, particularly the export sectors;

(b) to rehabilitate the country's productive base and economic and social infrastructure;

(c) to restore fiscal and monetary discipline; and

(d) to encourage private savings and investment.

A number of policy measures have been implemented to achieve these objectives. Among these are the following:

-   Exchange rate

The cedi was devalued in stages. During 1987-1990 there was a move to a market-determined exchange rate. (Table I). The exchange system was gradually liberalized and culminated in the establishment in 1988 of foreign exchange bureaux. In April 1990, an inter-bank foreign exchange market, supported by weekly wholesale auctions, was introduced. The real effective exchange rate depreciated by slightly over 20 per cent in 1987, by about 5 per cent in 1988 and 1989, and was unchanged in 1990. The differential between the auction and forex bureau rates has disappeared from a peak of 50 per cent in early 1989; and foreign exchange is now easily available (Table II). These reforms have been complemented by the liberalization of payments and transfers for current international transactions.

-   Export incentives

As incentives to production, actions that have been taken besides the exchange rate adjustments, include raising cocoa producer prices;

eliminating most restrictions on trade; and reforming the tax system. The rate of f.o.b. prices received by cocoa farmers rose from 23 per cent in the 1986/87 crop season to an estimated 47 per cent for the 1990/91 crop season. The increase reflected the adjustment to a more realistic exchange rate, reduction in the high costs of the Ghana Cocoa Board and a decrease in the excessive taxation of farmers. This showed a significant impact on production. Output rose sharply from 228,000 tonnes in 1986/87 to about 300,000 tonnes in 1988/89 and 1989/90, which indicates the virtual cessation of smuggling.

Since 1987 the level of Ghana's import tariffs have been lowered, and quantitative restrictions completely removed. In 1988 import and domestic sales taxes were realigned and the import licensing system abolished in 1989. Currently, Ghana's tariff structure generally ranges from zero to 25 per cent with special protective taxes ranging from 10-40 per cent on some dozen products. As mentioned earlier, super sales taxes on luxury goods introduced in the 1990 fiscal year, and ranging from 75-500 per cent, were lowered from 10-100 per cent during the 1991 fiscal year.

TABLE I

Summary of developments in the exchange rate system

-   Prior to 1983, Ghana had maintained a system of fixed exchange rates with the par value of the cedi at 2.75 to the dollar since 1978.

-   In 1983 a system of multiple exchange rates involving surcharges and subsidies was introduced and operated for only three months.

-   Return to fixed exchange with the cedi exchanging for ¢30 to the dollar.

-   In September 1986 dual exchange rate systems - windows I and II (administrative and auction respectively) were introduced. Transactions at window I related to official transactions and were pegged at ¢90 to the dollar. Window II rates were determined through weekly auctions. First rate determined at auction was ¢120 to US dollar.

-   February 1987 the windows merged and exchange rates were determined by auction.

-   In February 1988 "forex bureaux" were introduced. They determine their own sale and purchase prices.

-   Effective 29 December 1989 a wholesale foreign exchange auction introduced, permitting authorized dealer banks and eligible forex bureaux to purchase foreign exchange on behalf of their customers and on their own behalf.

TABLE II

Nominal and Real Exchange Rates, 1964-1989

	Official Exchange Rates			Parallel Exchange Rates			Ratio
Year	Official nominal rate (₵/$)	Index of official rate (84=100)	Index of real official (₵/$)	Parallel nominal rate (84=100)	Index of parallel rate (84=100)	Index of real parallel (84=100)	Parallel to nominal rate (per cent)
1964	0.714	1.96	246.70	1.18	1.22	153.86	165
1965	0.714	1.96	202.06	1.41	1.46	150.59	197
1966	0.714	1.96	183.15	1.38	1.43	133.59	193
1967.1	0.714	1.96	201.60	1.77	1.83	188.60	248
1967.2	0.714	1.96	194.87	1.77	1.83	182.31	248
1967.3	1.020	2.80	288.24	1.77	1.83	188.76	174
1967.4	1.020	2.80	284.61	1.77	1.83	186.38	174
1968	1.020	2.80	253.84	1.86	1.92	174.69	182
1970	1.020	2.80	244.91	1.69	1.75	153.14	166
1971	1.020	2.80	247.09	1.52	1.57	138.96	149
1972.1	1.820	4.99	460.89	1.68	1.74	160.55	92
1972.2	1.280	3.51	300.58	1.68	1.74	148.88	131
1972.3	1.280	3.51	310.97	1.68	1.74	154.03	131
1972.4	1.280	3.51	312.44	1.68	1.74	154.76	131
1973.1	1.210	3.32	301.52	1.50	1.55	141.06	124
1973.2	1.150	3.15	278.11	1.50	1.55	136.90	130
1973.3	1.150	3.15	271.16	1.50	1.55	133.47	130
1973.4	1.150	3.15	291.53	1.50	1.55	143.50	130
1974	1.150	3.15	279.03	1.73	1.79	158.41	150
1975	1.150	3.15	240.34	1.99	2.06	156.95	173
1976	1.150	3.15	154.12	2.91	3.01	141.91	253
1977	1.150	3.15	83.61	9.20	9.52	250.18	800
1978.1	1.150	3.15	65.78	6.98	7.22	150.67	607
1978.2	1.175	3.22	56.91	8.84	9.14	161.59	752
1978.3	1.979	5.42	93.07	10.00	10.34	177.48	505
1978.4	2.750	7.54	106.33	10.00	10.34	145.91	364
1979	2.750	7.54	96.14	15.56	16.10	209.89	566
1980	2.750	7.54	75.76	15.87	16.41	165.20	577
1981	2.750	7.54	33.78	26.25	27.15	120.23	955
1982	2.750	7.54	25.67	61.67	63.79	209.61	2,242
1983.1	2.750	7.54	16.93	76.67	79.31	178.17	2,788
1983.2	24.690	67.68	96.32	60.67	62.76	89.32	246
1983.3	24.690	67.68	90.17	78.33	81.03	107.96	317
1983.4	30.000	82.24	97.08	90.67	93.80	110.73	302
1984.1	30.300	83.06	85.44	93.00	96.21	98.96	307
1984.2	35.000	95.94	92.70	97.00	100.34	96.96	277
1984.3	38.500	105.54	107.31	97.00	100.34	102.03	252
1984.4	42.120	115.46	115.36	99.67	103.11	103.02	237
1985.1	50.000	137.06	117.90	128.33	132.75	114.20	257
1985.2	53.000	145.28	127.65	129.00	133.45	117.25	243
1985.3	57.000	156.25	145.60	131.67	136.21	126.93	231
1985.4	60.000	164.47	159.90	136.00	140.69	136.78	227

TABLE II (cont'd)

| Year | Official Exchange Rates | | | Parallel Exchange Rates | | | Ratio |
	Official nominal rate (¢/$)	Index of official rate (84=100)	Index of real official (¢/$)	Parallel nominal rate (84=100)	Index of parallel rate (84=100)	Index of real parallel (84=100)	Parallel to nominal rate (percent)
1986.1	90.000	246.71	225.92				
1986.2	90.000	246.71	218.53				
1986.3	90.000	246.71	222.38	200.00	206.89	186.50	222
1986.4	149.417	409.58	335.54	192.50	199.14	163.14	129
1987.1	152.636	418.40	321.92	201.82	208.78	160.63	132
1987.2	158.364	434.10	308.08	226.36	234.17	166.18	143
1987.3	165.077	452.50	307.61	251.54	260.21	176.89	152
1987.4	174.333	477.88	342.37	260.00	268.96	192.70	149
1988.1	180.667	495.24	326.63				
1988.2	185.833	509.40	302.14				
1988.3	217.231	595.47	327.65				
1988.4	230.083	630.70	365.27				
1989.1	245.350	672.55	351.99				

Notes: Real exchange rates calculated as the product of the nominal rate and the ratio of a trade-weighted world wholesale price index to the Ghanian CPI. Weights are constructed using Ghana's six largest trading partners, exclusive of Nigeria, during the 1980-1984 period (see Edwards, Chapter 4, for a discussion of an alternative definition).

All annual rates are arithmetic averages of reported quarterly figures.

Beginning with 1986.4, quarterly official nominal exchange rates are calculated as the arithmetic average of the relevant weekly rates established in the official foreign exchange auction. Similarly, the nominal parallel rate after 1986.3 is the average of the weekly rates established in the (legal) private foreign exchange bureaux.

Source: Nominal official Ghanaian exchange rates through 1986.3, as well as trade statistics, the Ghanaian CPI, and price indices and official nominal exchange rates of trading partners, are from IMF, International Financial Statistics (various years).

Parallel exchange rates through 1986.3 from Pick's Yearbook.

The tax structure has also been reformed. Over the period 1987-1990, consumption taxation (on petroleum and motor vehicles) was expanded; taxes were consolidated and tax administration improved. There was more relief for personal income taxes and some of the loopholes relating to allowances were closed. Tax on cocoa was lowered and corporate taxes reduced (from 55 per cent to 45 per cent for manufacturing, construction, farming and export, and to 50 per cent for all other sectors). There was a further reduction in the 1991 budget from 45 per cent to 35 per cent in the corporate tax rate, in the withholding tax on dividends from 30 per cent to 15 per cent, and the extension of the capital allowance provided under the Investment Code to all enterprises in the manufacturing sector. Wide ranging reliefs have been further granted in personal income tax rates.

As an incentive to the export sector, corporate tax rebates have also been raised from a minimum range of 30 per cent to 40 per cent, to a maximum of 60 per cent to 75 per cent for agriculture, and in the case of manufacturing, from a minimum range of 25 per cent to 30 per cent to a maximum of 60 per cent to 75 per cent, depending on the proportion of output exported. The duty drawback has also been increased from 95 per cent to 100 per cent.

These tax measures are a part of a renewed effort to revitalize the private sector through a stimulation of private savings and investment. The government is aware that these measures will no doubt have some adverse effects on revenues but expects them to spur investments, create employment and thereby compensate for any short-term revenue loss.

-    Public resource management

In public resource management there have been considerable improvements in government revenue mobilization and reduction in budget deficits. This has been made possible by drastically streamlining and rationalizing expenditure. A three-year rolling Public Investment Programme (PIP) has been prepared to rehabilitate economic and social infrastructure, including cocoa, timber and the mining sectors, with increased budget support for education and health. Planned public sector investment in 1990 continued to concentrate on infrastructure (58%). Outlays on social sectors accounted for nearly 20 per cent of the programme. Ninety-five per cent of expenditures were from budgetary sources.

Much progress has been made in reforming the pay structure and reducing overstaffing in the Civil Service and the Ghana Education Service. For instance, a total of 13,937 civil servants, primarily surplus unskilled staff were redeployed during 1989. Net redeployment was, however, 10,521 if account is taken of the additional recruitment that took place.

Progress has also been made in the <u>reform of the State-owned enterprises (SOEs)</u>. The main objectives of the reform which began in 1987 were to reduce the size of the sector through divestiture and to improve the efficiency of priority enterprises through the monitoring of agreed targets based on corporate plans and associated performance agreements.

As at the end of January 1991, a total of 38 enterprises had been divested, of which 23 were liquidations of negligible, inactive companies and 15 were privatizations (including joint-ventures, management contacts, leases and sales of shares). Capacity to use the corporate plans and performance contracts as an instrument to improve the operations of State enterprises has increased. For instance, eight out of thirteen SOEs with corporate plans increased their profits (after interest and taxes) from 0.5 per cent of GDP in 1988 to 1.5 per cent of GDP in 1989.

- ## Financial sector reforms

In order to strengthen the financial system to support the adjustment programme, the Government has embarked on financial sector reforms. This is to enable investors to respond to the improved incentives and enable mobilization of savings. The reforms which began in 1988 comprised, among others, enactment of a new Banking Law (PNDC Law 225) which came into force in August 1989, and established prudential banking provisions; introduced uniform accounting and auditing standards and improved reporting requirements to the Bank of Ghana; a strengthening of the Bank of Ghana's supervisory capacity; and a phased programme of bank restructuring involving the replacement of non-performing assets with performing assets, primarily bonds. The restructuring was completed in early 1991 and the banking sector is now better able to respond to the demands for credit from the private sector.

- ## Corporate restructuring

A corporate restructuring programme to revive real sector activities, particularly in the manufacturing sector has been launched. A corporate restructuring company, the First Finance Company Limited (FFCL), has been established to undertake corporate restructuring on behalf of institutional creditors and other holders of corporate debt; and to assist individuals and institutional investors in restructuring the firms' operations, financial arrangements and management. It is also to promote investment and may itself invest in these firms. The FFCL is expected to be funded from both local and foreign sources.

- ## Legal and regulatory framework

In order to make the legal and regulatory framework reflect the policy reforms, which are aimed at creating a market-oriented economy in which the private sector plays a leading rôle, the government has appointed an advisory group, the Chairman and the majority of whose members are from the private sector, to review and make proposals for appropriate changes in existing laws to make them consistent with the liberalizing and deregulating thrust of the policy reforms.

- PAMSCAD

Besides all this, a special programme of action to mitigate the social costs of adjustment (PAMSCAD) has also been launched. This involves mainly financial support for community-initiated projects and credit lines to small scale enterprises and peasant farmers. Efforts have also been made to widen local participation in decision-making through elected district assemblies and the drafting of a new constitution in preparation for a return to constitutional rule.

- <u>Needs and new policy directions</u>

Evidently there has been much progress towards restoring macro-economic balance. Various economic and social indexes have shown that economic performance since the launching of the reforms, which have received considerable support since 1987 by the Structural Adjustment Credit (SAC) facility of the International Development Association (IDA), has generally been satisfactory.

TABLE III

Key Financial Rates and Ratios

Year end	Discount rate	Deposit rate	Lending rate	Inflation rate	Exchange rate ($/¢)	Liquidity Minimum	Ratio Actual
1960	4.0	3.0	7.5	0.9	1.400	45	77.5
1961	4.5	3.5	7.0	6.2	1.400	54	47.3
1962	4.5	3.5	7.0	5.9	1.400	50	55.0
1963	4.5	3.5	7.0	5.6	1.400	54	36.3
1964	4.5	3.5	7.0	15.8	1.400	54	70.0
1965	4.5	3.5	7.0	22.7	1.400	54	60.8
1966	7.0	3.5	9.0	14.8	1.400	54	78.7
1967	6.0	3.5	9.0	-9.7	0.980	54	66.5
1968	5.5	3.5	9.0	10.7	0.980	54	71.3
1969	5.5	3.5	9.0	6.5	0.980	35	60.9
1970	5.5	3.5	9.0	3.0	0.980	50	58.4
1971	8.0	7.5	9.0	8.0	0.550	40	50.9
1972	8.0	7.5	12.0	10.8	0.781	40	63.1
1973	6.0	5.0	10.0	17.1	0.870	40	60.5
1974	6.0	5.0	10.0	18.8	0.870	40	46.8
1975	8.0	7.5	12.5	29.8	0.870	40	57.0
1976	8.0	7.5	12.5	55.4	0.870	40	56.4
1977	8.0	7.5	12.5	116.5	0.870	67	62.4
1978	13.5	11.5	19.0	73.1	0.364	67	79.4
1979	13.5	11.5	19.0	54.5	0.364	67	89.1
1980	13.5	11.5	19.0	50.2	0.364	67	80.7
1981	19.5	11.5	19.0	116.5	0.364	60	80.0
1982	10.5	11.5	19.0	22.3	0.364	60	77.3
1983	14.5	11.5	19.0	122.8	0.033	45	79.1
1984	18.0	15.0	21.17	39.7	0.020	45	63.9
1985	18.5	15.75	21.17	10.3	0.017	40	65.4
1986	20.5	17.0	20.0	24.6	0.011	34	63.5
1987	23.5	17.58	25.5	39.8	0.006	29	40.8
1988	26.0	16.0	25.58	31.4	0.005	30	42.0

Source: Bank of Ghana, Annual Reports, various issues; quarterly digest of statistics, June 1989 and International Financial Statistics, 1988 Yearbook.

Between 1983 and 1989 the real GDP grew at an average of almost 6 per cent a year; there has been appreciable growth in exports; the rate of inflation (as measured by the changes in the national consumer price index) decelerated from about 123 per cent in 1983 to 25 per cent in 1989; and the overall balance of payments switched from a large deficit in 1985 and 1986 to a sizeable surplus (Table III and Appendix I).

However, much remains to be accomplished. For, in spite of this improved performance inflation rates and current account deficits remain high; domestic savings and investments are still low to allow a sustainable expansion in output without excessive dependence on external concessional assistance; the financial intermediation process is still weak; the position of the State enterprise sector in the economy continues to be weak; the external position remains vulnerable to adverse developments in world prices for cocoa, gold and petroleum products; the complexity and limited transparency of the legal and administrative framework remain; tax distortions appear to be impeding a stronger expansion in private sector activity; and the private sector response to the improved macro-economic environment has been modest. Also, human resource development, poverty and environmental issues need to be addressed. There is a serious problem of implementation as the public sector's management capacity has been strained by the increasing demands generated by the reforms.

Medium-term programme objectives

Given this backdrop, the objectives during the SAC III period (1991-93) have been designed to address the above problems and they include:

(a) to achieve an annual rate of real GDP growth of about 5 per cent;

(b) to reduce the average inflation rate from about 37 per cent in 1990 to 5 per cent by 1993;

(c) to continue to generate sizeable overall balance-of-payments surpluses averaging about US$90 million a year so as to reduce reliance on external assistance; and

(d) to ensure that the gains of adjustment reflect in living standards by enhancing employment opportunities.

Obviously, the achievement of these objectives will entail further increases in domestic savings and investment, especially in the private sector, and a greater diversification of the export base to be facilitated by an accelerated institutional and structural reform.

To these ends the programme for 1991-1993 has as its main elements the following:

(a) continued tight financial policies;

(b) further improvements in incentives to produce, save and invest, including the maintenance of a broadly stable, real effective exchange rate, tax reforms and flexible agricultural producer prices. Private sector investment promotion will accordingly be accorded the highest priority;

(c) diversification into processed and manufactured exports in order to reduce the economy's vulnerability to an uncertain external environment, as regards commodity prices;

(d)   a reinforcement of monetary policies and a shift towards increased reliance on open-market-type liquidity management;

(e)   an enhancement of the effectiveness of the financial intermediation process through accelerated implementation of the bank restructuring programme and of financial sector reform in general;

(f)   measures to strengthen further the efficiency and equity of the tax system, including the rationalization of the structure of taxes on capital and investment income;

(g)   higher public investment for the rehabilitation of the basic economic and social infrastructure combined with adequate provisions for recurrent spending;

(h)   acceleration of State enterprise reform, in particular of the divestiture programme; and improvement in public sector management, including measures to improve the quality of human capital; and

(i)   further restructuring of import duties in stages, to create a lower and more uniform pattern of production to encourage the development of non-traditional exports and efficient import substitution industries. This will involve lower standard rates, and a phasing-out of special import taxes, further reducing the scope of duty exemptions and concessions and streamlining the duty drawback system. The Government expects by the end of 1991 a study to be completed on the effects of trade liberalization on the manufacturing sector, and will establish procedures for reviewing rates of duty on particular products and responding to requests for changes in protection.

These policies will continue to be complemented with appropriate sectoral strategies indicated in A(i) above, notably in agriculture, industry, health and education as well as efforts to protect the environment.

One of the principal objectives of the programme is to ensure that policy reforms are implemented on schedule so as to be mutually supportive and to minimize adjustment costs.

Needs

Ghana's external requirements to implement the programme in the medium-term are detailed in Appendix III.

(ii)   The external economic environment

(a) Major trends in imports and exports

Imports

One of the initial developments in the implementation of the ERP was the use of prudent import management practices as one of the instruments for addressing the balance-of-payments problem. At the same time it was realized that export growth required liberalization of imports. Measures which have influenced imports since 1983, therefore, include:

-    the abolition of import licensing;

-    liberalization of foreign exchange remittance to facilitate importation of goods from "own resources";

-    introduction of the foreign exchange auction system; and

-    introduction of the forex bureau system which allows foreign exchange to be freely bought and sold.

From 1983-1985 there was a yearly rise in imports. Between 1986 and 1988, however, following the various incentives for the export sector, including the liberalization measures, exports outstripped imports, with imports again outgrowing exports in 1989, albeit slowly, and rebounding in 1990 (Figure I).

In the future import volume is expected to grow in line with the growth in the economy. Growth in petroleum demand is projected to slow down in response to the higher excise taxes. The implementation of the medium-term Agricultural Development Programme is expected to increase food production and thereby moderate the growth in food imports. As interest obligations to the IMF are expected to ease and as most of the medium-term loans have been paid off, net factor payments are projected to fall.

Exports

The importance of exports in the Ghanaian economy is evident in the relative high proportion of the value of export earnings in Ghana's GNP which accounted for approximately 20 per cent in 1979, 20 per cent in 1985 and 15 per cent in 1986. The main source of Ghana's export earnings has been cocoa, minerals and timber (Table IV and Figure II).

TABLE IV

Exports (Value, Volume and Unit Price of Exports, 1983-90)

	1983	1984	1985	1986	1987	1988	1989	1990
Cocoa beans ($'M)	242.11	351.69	375.97	469.81	451.02	422.26	381.31	323.82
Volume (metric tonnes)	159,280	149,574	171,747	195,224	197,988	200,904	225,860	247,380
Unit price ($/tonne)	1,520.00	2,351.30	2,189.10	2,406.50	2,278.00	2,101.80	1,490.30	1,309
Cocoa products ($'M)	26.50	30.00	36.02	33.50	44.40	39.78	26.45	36.80
Volume (metric tonnes)	15,000	15,265	15,966	15,645	20,983	20,250.00	14,940	20,756
Unit price ($/tonne)	1,766.70	1,965.30	2,256.20	2,141.30	2,116.00	1,964.60	1,770.40	1,773
Gold ($'M)	114.09	103.27	90.62	106.39	142.50	168.52	159.94	201.65
Volume (fine ounces)	278,000	285,759	285,138	292,211	323,496	382,993	420,096	526,361
Unit price ($/fine ounce)	410.40	361.40	317.80	364.10	440.50	440.00	380.70	383.1
Diamond ($'M)	2.81	2.81	5.50	4.80	3.97	3.52	5.23	16.55
Volume (carat)	439,000	425,035	639,593	564,950	396,720	305,787	262,691	636,371
Unit price ($/carat)	6.40	6.60	8.60	8.50	10.00	11.50	19.90	26.0
Bauxite ($'M)	1.68	0.92	2.74	5.00	5.21	6.90	9.15	9.95
Volume (metric tonnes)	82,000	45,000	124,453	226,461	226,415	299,939	374,646	368,629
Unit price ($/tonne)	20.50	20.50	22.00	22.10	23.00	23.00	24.40	27.0
Manganese ($'M)	3.10	8.30	9.04	8.21	7.76	8.75	11.69	14.22
Volume (metric tonnes)	127,000	247,784	263,441	245,794	235,123	282,337	284,645	255,310
Unit price ($/tonne)	24.40	33.50	34.30	33.40	33.00	31.00	41.10	55.7
Timber ($'M)	14.69	21.20	27.79	44.09	89.82	106.21	80.20	117.99
Volume (cubic metres)	103,303	148,252	246,812	291,382	493,543	545,778	375,826	370,000
Unit price ($/cubic metre)	142.20	143.00	112.60	151.30	182.00	194.60	213.40	318.9
Residual oil ($'M)	21.10	22.60	33.42	17.59	19.11	16.87	19.54	28.64
Volume (metric tonnes)	112,000	124,445	198,837	202,216	169,071	206,019	216,616	227,472
Unit price ($/tonne)	188.40	181.60	168.10	87.00	113.00	81.90	90.20	125.9
Electricity	11.80	20.80	34.50	45.90	49.30	73.60	82.48	88.37
Coffee ($'M)	0.00	1.30	0.69	1.20	1.20	0.92	0.85	0.58
Volume (metric tonnes)		554	280	458	635	600	675	680
Unit price ($/tonne)		2,346.60	2,449.70	2,617.80	1,892.00	1,530.00	1,259.30	853.0
Sheanut ($'M)	0.40	0.17	8.69	8.40	2.91	2.72	0.38	1.32
Volume (metric tonnes)		399	17,000	23,750	9,000	20,000	2,235	4,171
Unit price ($/tonne)		426.00	511.30	353.70	323.00	136.00	170.02	316.0
Other non-traditional	1.00	2.80	7.50	4.40	9.60	30.92	30.92	50.67
Total exports	439.28	565.86	632.48	749.30	826.79	880.97	807.22	890.56

Source: Bank of Ghana

Against this background, an important objective of the ERP in the export sector has been the accelerated expansion and diversification of exports. During the period 1983-1988 export earnings rose from US$460 million to US$869 million (nearly a 90 per cent increase). Earnings in 1989 were US$880 million.

There is now evidence that exports have significantly responded to the exchange rate and various trade policy reforms as well as the incentive schemes. However, exports are still too narrowly based with cocoa and gold accounting for almost 70 per cent of total export earnings. In 1983, 278,000 ounces of gold valued at about US$114 million were produced; by 1990 gold output had almost doubled to about US$201 million. There are indications that by 1995 gold would have achieved rough parity in earnings with cocoa.

There has also been a reasonably strong growth in non-traditional exports. These increased in value from US$24 million in 1986 to US$42 million in 1988, declined to US$35 million in 1989, and are estimated to have increased very significantly to US$62 million in 1990.

Potential exists for expanding the non-traditional exports sector, particularly the agricultural non-traditional exports, such as pineapples, kola nuts, tuna, fish, vegetables and flowers. In the area of semi-processed and manufactured exports, furniture, other wood products and processed fruits hold the best medium-term prospects, while salt and aluminium products have especially good prospects within the West African sub-region.

Prospects

Led primarily by earnings from gold, export earnings are projected to grow at an average annual rate of about 11 per cent compared with the stagnation experienced between 1988 and 1990. The combination of higher production and a modest recovery in international prices is expected to account for the projected growth in export earnings. The share of cocoa in total exports, which has fallen from 51 per cent in 1989 to 41 per cent in 1990, is expected to continue to fall, reaching around 30 per cent by 1995.

The opening-up of new mines and rehabilitation of existing ones are expected to result in an average annual growth rate in gold exports of about 18 per cent between 1990 and 1995.

As a result of policies to protect the environment and preserve Ghana's forests, the growth rates for exports of logs and other timber products are expected to be around 3 per cent per annum. However, with expected shifts to value-added timber products, some improvements in unit price are projected. It is expected, therefore, that the share of timber in total exports will increase gradually from less than 10 per cent in 1989 to about 15 per cent in 1995.

Figure I
Ghana's External Trade (Exports/Imports), 1983-89

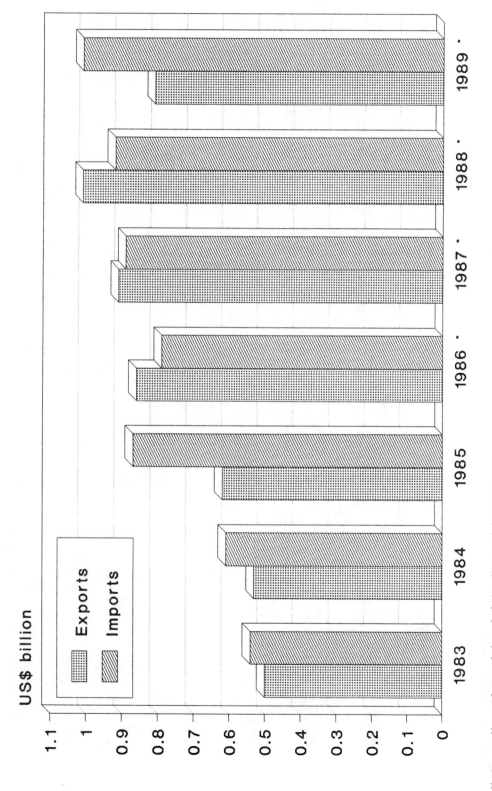

US$ billion

Exports

Imports

1983 1984 1985 1986 * 1987 * 1988 * 1989 *

1.1 1 0.9 0.8 0.7 0.6 0.5 0.4 0.3 0.2 0.1 0

Note: Use of provisional data denoted by asterisk.

Source: Ministry of Trade, Bank of Ghana, Statistical Service.

Figure II
Major Sectors' Performance of Exports, 1983-89

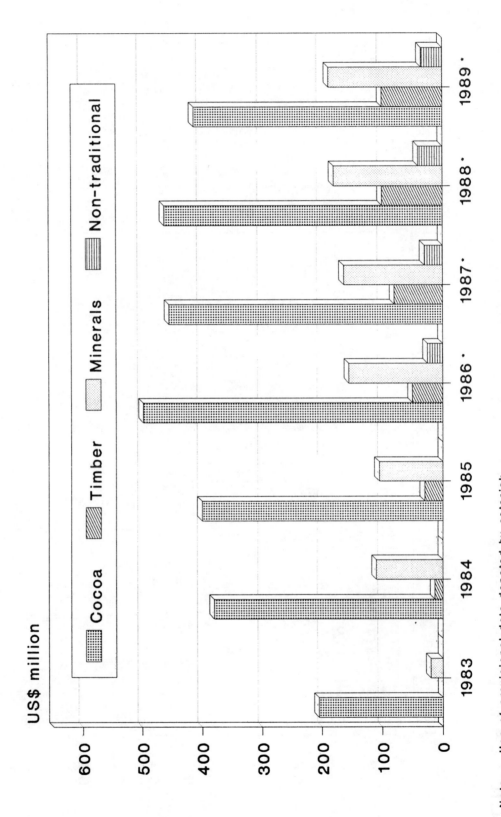

Note: Use of provisional data denoted by asterisk.

Source: Ministry of Trade, Bank of Ghana, Statistical Service.

Also, the share of non-traditional exports whose volume increased sharply in 1990 and showed a growth of about 12 per cent, is projected to increase from 4 per cent in 1989 to around 7 per cent in 1993.

(b)   Developments in the terms of trade and commodity prices

Even though the external environment was broadly favourable during 1983-86, Ghana's terms of trade deteriorated by 8.3 per cent in 1987, 9.0 per cent in 1988 and by 17.2 per cent and 14.3 per cent in 1989 and 1990, respectively (Appendix III).   This was due mainly to declines in world prices for Ghana's cocoa and gold during the period as well as the sharp increase in oil prices in August 1990.   The deterioration of 17.5 per cent in 1989 is estimated to have been substantially more than the average for all Sub-Saharan African countries.   As a result, export earnings increased at a more moderate rate.   Between 1987 and 1990, export earnings increased on average by 2.5 per cent compared with an average increase of about 20 per cent during the three preceding years.   New investments and the rehabilitation of existing operations in gold mining resulted in the share of gold earnings increasing from 17 per cent in 1987 to 23 per cent in 1990.   Gold earnings would have been even greater but for the falling international prices.

Timber exports picked up markedly in 1990 due to a shift in exports of processed timber.   Notwithstanding a cumulative deterioration in the terms of trade by more than 30 per cent during 1988-1990, Ghana's balance of payments continued to strengthen, registering overall surpluses of US$124.6 million in 1988, US$127.4 million in 1989 and US$85.0 million in 1990.

This favourable development was made possible, on the one hand, by a marked recovery of non-cocoa exports resulting from the rehabilitation of several export-oriented sectors and, on the other hand, by a sharp increase in external assistance from bilateral and multilateral sources.

Ghana's terms of trade are projected to improve by about 10 per cent between 1990 and 1995, though this position will still be about 25 per cent worse than in 1986-87.   The improvement in the balance-of-payments position is to come from volume increases in exports, changes in composition towards higher value-added products and continued prudent demand management, as well as the maintenance of a competitive exchange rate.

(c)   Important trends in the balance of payments, reserves, debt, exchange and interest rates, and other such issues

-   Balance of payments

Following the developments in terms of trade mentioned in (b) above, Ghana's balance of payments continued to be weak between 1983 and 1986, and overall balances for each year during the period, except for 1984, was negative (Appendix I). However, surpluses have been registered since 1987 in spite of the adverse terms of trade.

The balance-of-payments position in 1989 and 1990 was adversely affected by the weakening of the world prices for cocoa. The price per metric ton averaged US$1,372 in 1989-90, as compared with US$2,190 in 1987-88. Cocoa earnings amounted to about US$357.1 million in 1990, down from US$407.8 in 1989. Cocoa output was about the same in the two years, around 280,000 metric tonnes, but the decline in revenue was brought about by a 19 per cent decline in average export price in 1990 relative to 1989. The value of merchandise exports for 1990 is provisionally put at US$825.7 million. This represents a nominal increase of 2.3 per cent over the 1989 figure of US$807.2 million. The slight improvement in the earnings in 1990 relative to 1989 was due mainly to an increase in gold earnings from US$159.9 million in 1989 to US$196.6 million in 1990. Other exports (mainly manganese, residual oil and diamonds) also registered an increase in earnings from US$159.3 million in 1989 to US$186.3 million in 1990.

The current account deficit (including official transfers) widened from US$82.8 million in 1989 to US$258.9 million in 1990, but a positive net capital account position due to increase in external assistance produced an overall surplus of US$85 million in 1990. Although the 1990 surplus was lower than the 1989 surplus of US$127.4 million, it nevertheless enabled the retirement of payments arrears to the tune of US$17.3 million in 1990, such that by the end of June 1990, Ghana had no official payments arrears.

Projections

On the basis of a programmed average annual increase of about 4.7 per cent in the volume of non-oil imports, Ghana's trade deficit is expected to widen further to US$364 million in 1991 and to decline to US$314 by 1993, averaging US$327 million a year during 1991-93.

Over the same period, the services account is projected to register net outflows averaging US$383 million. With external interest payments averaging US$117 million taking into account the recent debt cancellations by some bilateral creditors, partly in response to the more realistic exchange rate, the improved confidence in the banking system, and the improved macro economic environment, inflows of private transfers are projected to an average of US$200 million a year. As a result the current account deficit, excluding net official transfers, is projected to increase to US$514 million in 1991 and to decline to US$491 million by 1993. As a percentage of GNP this implies a progressive narrowing of the current account deficit from 8.3 per cent in 1990 to 6.0 per cent in 1993.

Based on existing pipeline concessional assistance and new commitments, disbursements of official grants and long-term loans from both bilateral and multilateral sources are expected to average about US$630 million a year during 1991-93.

108. Taking account of amortization due and the other net capital flows, Ghana's balance of payments are projected to record overall surpluses averaging US$90 million a year. This would cover the scheduled repayments to the Fund, while allowing for a significant accumulation of gross official reserves. The expected improvement in the balance of payments by the end of 1991 would enable Ghana in subsequent years to do without Fund resources and other foreign financing for balance-of-payments support. It would also reduce Ghana's reliance on external concessional assistance over the medium term.

-   The exchange rate

As indicated in Tables I and II, prior to 1983 Ghana had maintained a system of fixed exchange rates with the par value of the cedi at ¢2.75 to one US dollar. This rate had prevailed since 1978. In 1983 a multiple exchange rate system was introduced involving surcharges and subsidies, which operated for only three months. There was a return to the fixed exchange rate but this time the cedi exchanged for ¢30 to one US dollar.

A fundamental change was introduced in September 1986 with the introduction of the two-tier exchange rate system. The system comprised two exchange rates, one of which was administratively determined and the other through a weekly foreign exchange auction. Another step towards the further liberalization of the trade and exchange rate system was the authorization of the establishment in February 1988 of Forex bureaux by individuals, companies and banks for the purchase and sale of foreign exchange.

In the pursuit of the ultimate goal of achieving a market-determined and realistic exchange rate based on a unified foreign exchange market, a wholesale foreign exchange auction was introduced in December 1989 which permitted authorized dealer banks and eligible Forex bureaux to purchase foreign exchange from the Bank of Ghana for their customers, and also on their own behalf to meet their import requirements. Effective 27 April 1990 the wholesale auction was modified to permit authorized dealer banks and eligible Forex bureaux to purchase foreign exchange from the Bank of Ghana as principals for sale to their end-user customers and also to meet their own foreign exchange needs.

Currently, authorized dealer banks and eligible Forex bureaux are permitted to trade in foreign exchange among themselves or with other customers, provided the foreign exchange traded in is not subject to surrender requirements.

Following on from these developments, increased convergence was achieved during 1989 and early 1990 between the foreign exchange bureau and auction rates, primarily through an increased supply of foreign exchange through the retail auction, thereby reducing the excess demand that previously spilled over to the bureaux. As a result, the foreign exchange bureau rates remained broadly stable while the pace of depreciation of the auction rate accelerated. The spread between the average buying bureau rate and the auction rate (as a percentage of the latter) declined markedly from a peak of about 40 per cent to some 8 per cent by late April 1990. This spread has since been practically eliminated, especially if account is taken of the commissions charged by the authorized dealers.

With the unification of the auction and foreign exchange bureau markets on 27 April 1990, and the lifting at the same time of the remaining minor exchange restrictions relating to invisible payments, there is now a full liberalization of payments and transfers for current international transactions. The unified exchange market has been functioning relatively smoothly, ensuring an increased and efficient availability of foreign exchange for development and growth. The pace of depreciation of the nominal effective exchange rate slowed down markedly to 9.3 per cent during 1989 and 9.0 per cent during the first three quarters of 1990, thus contributing to a stable real effective exchange rate. (A summary of purchases and sales in the auction and foreign exchange bureau markets is provided in Table V).

- Interest rates

All interest rates were decontrolled and liberalized in 1988 and since then banks have been free to fix their borrowing and lending rates. All bank charges, except charges on turnover, were decontrolled during the last quarter of 1990, and all banks are now free to fix their own charges. However, bank deposit and lending rates remained virtually unchanged at levels significantly negative in real terms (Table III). In late 1990, the Government implemented a number of major policy measures with a view to strengthening the response of market interest rates to changes in the liquidity conditions of the economy, enhancing the transparency and efficiency of the process of auctioning financial instruments, and giving the right signals to the private sector.

These measures included:

(i)   an increase in the rediscount rate of the Bank of Ghana from 26 per cent to 35 per cent;

(ii)   an increase of about 5 percentage points in money market interest rates, induced by intensified open market operations; and

(iii)   the remuneration of bank cash deposits with the Bank of
         Ghana at an interest rate of 3 per cent.

These measures, combined with continued restrained credit expansion, led to
a further deceleration of the broad money supply to an estimated
17.5 per cent by the end of 1990.

It is the determination of the Government to restore and maintain
positive real interest rates, and thereby encourage the mobilization of
financial savings, by maintaining appropriately tight liquidity conditions
in the economy.

TABLE V

Summary of Purchases and Sales in
the Forex Exchange Auction Market

1. All Forex bureaux

(US$ million)

	1988 (Apr-Dec)	1989	1990	1991 (Jan-Mar)
Total purchases	51,477	123,269	221,278	75,682
Monthly average purchases	5,720	10,272	18,440	25,227
Total sales	50,572	116,328	220,411	73,073
Monthly average sales	5,619	9,694	18,368	24,358

2. Banks Forex bureaux

(US$ million)

	1988 (Apr-Dec)	1989	1990	1991 (Jan-Mar)
Total purchases	14,109	53,482	118,242	45,878
Monthly average purchases	2,016	4,457	9,854	15,293
Total sales	11,031	52,791	118,858	44,936
Monthly average sales	1,576	4,399	9,905	14,979

3. Non-bank bureaux

(US$ million)

	1988 (Apr-Dec)	1989	1990	1991 (Jan-Mar)
Total purchases	37,368	69,787	103,037	29,804
Monthly average purchases	4,152	5,816	8,586	9,935
Total sales	39,541	63,537	101,553	28,137
Monthly average sales	4,393	5,295	8,463	9,379

TABLE V (cont.)

Summary of Purchases and Sales of Foreign Exchange

in the Forex Bureau Market

Period	Purchases (US$)			Sales (US$)		
	A. Banks' bureaux	B. Non-bank bureaux	Total (A+B)	C. Banks' bureaux	D. Non-bank bureaux	Total (C+D)
1988						
April	0.00	517,325.00	517,325.00	0.00	573,946.00	573,946.00
May	0.00	2,181,533.00	2,181,533.00	0.00	2,043,837.00	2,043,837.00
June	205,319.00	2,852,716.00	3,058,035.00	163,731.00	2,763,600.00	2,927,331.00
July	459,236.00	5,313,388.00	5,772,624.00	336,609.00	5,051,750.00	5,388,359.00
August	1,711,914.00	5,275,553.00	6,987,467.00	1,458,823.00	6,234,222.00	7,693,045.00
September	1,198,743.00	4,291,457.00	6,210,200.00	1,791,286.00	4,876,405.00	6,667,691.00
October	1,447,289.00	5,323,156.00	6,770,445.00	895,801.00	5,582,618.00	6,478,419.00
November	3,277,796.00	6,937,668.00	10,215,464.00	2,844,023.00	6,998,244.00	9,842,267.00
December	5,088,763.00	4,675,567.00	9,764,330.00	3,540,866.00	5,416,269.00	8,957,135.00
Total	14,109,060.00	37,368,363.00	51,477,423.00	11,031,139.00	39,540,891.00	50,572,030.00
1989						
January	2,448,612.00	6,999,535.00	9,448,147.00	2,686,176.00	6,428,657.00	9,114,833.00
February	4,032,933.00	5,576,207.00	9,609,140.00	5,206,287.00	3,653,913.00	8,860,200.00
March	5,669,055.00	5,718,707.00	11,387,762.00	4,488,618.00	5,621,050.00	10,109,668.00
April	4,824,361.00	7,095,960.00	11,920,321.00	3,045,890.00	6,625,376.00	9,671,266.00
May	4,341,018.00	5,092,197.00	9,433,215.00	3,780,572.00	5,164,832.00	8,945,404.00
June	2,771,136.00	9,200,661.00	11,971,797.00	3,324,170.00	7,493,415.00	10,817,585.00
July	3,428,132.00	4,222,489.00	7,650,621.00	4,078,691.00	4,477,307.00	8,555,998.00
August	6,998,501.00	3,868,006.00	10,866,507.00	5,963,734.00	3,704,950.00	9,668,684.00
September	2,761,865.00	4,144,958.00	6,906,823.00	3,514,778.00	2,420,624.00	5,935,402.00
October	1,873,492.00	8,573,003.00	10,446,495.00	2,714,334.00	8,373,158.00	11,087,492.00
November	6,012,396.00	4,447,379.00	10,459,775.00	6,417,615.00	4,995,594.00	11,413,209.00
December	8,320,248.00	4,848,201.00	13,168,449.00	7,570,472.00	4,578,259.00	12,148,734.00
Total	53,481,749.00	69,787,303.00	123,269,052.00	52,791,337.00	63,537,135.00	116,328,472.00
1990						
January	5,654,150.00	7,972,216.00	13,626,366.00	8,288,971.00	7,915,159.00	16,204,130.00
February	6,875,508.00	7,325,787.00	14,201,295.00	5,994,695.00	7,163,078.00	13,157,773.00
March	4,592,246.00	6,767,826.00	11,360,072.00	5,130,081.00	6,702,240.00	11,832,321.00
April	8,087,448.00	6,634,779.00	14,722,227.00	6,528,847.00	6,441,985.00	12,970,832.00
May	7,741,439.00	7,546,545.00	15,287,984.00	6,982,511.00	7,152,724.00	14,135,235.00
June	9,271,168.00	7,177,742.00	16,448,910.00	9,315,903.00	7,412,030.00	16,727,933.00
July	10,778,065.00	7,713,266.00	18,491,331.00	10,962,031.00	7,328,262.00	18,290,293.00
August	10,758,119.00	9,783,099.00	20,541,218.00	10,710,348.00	9,096,821.00	19,807,169.00
September	12,032,736.00	7,527,756.00	19,560,492.00	11,990,004.00	7,418,850.00	19,408,854.00
October	14,978,902.00	9,837,754.00	24,816,656.00	14,355,095.00	10,726,804.00	25,081,899.00
November	15,004,570.00	13,517,592.00	28,522,162.00	16,251,137.00	13,160,728.00	29,411,865.00
December	12,467,304.00	11,232,373.00	23,699,677.00	12,348,641.00	11,034,278.00	23,382,919.00
Total	118,241,655.00	103,036,735.00	221,278,390.00	118,858,264.00	101,552,959.00	220,411,223.00
1991						
January	17,761,750.00	10,217,052.00	27,978,802.00	18,581,800.00	9,951,216.00	28,533,016.00
February	14,880,126.00	9,827,529.00	24,707,655.00	14,220,860.00	9,108,261.00	23,329,121.00
March	13,236,321.00	9,759,398.00	22,995,719.00	12,133,552.00	9,077,352.00	21,210,904.00
Total	45,878,197.00	29,803,979.00	75,682,176.00	44,936,212.00	28,136,829.00	73,073,041.00

Source: Bank of Ghana

-    **External debt**

Total external debt is estimated to have fallen in absolute terms to US$2.9 billion by end 1989, equivalent to 55 per cent of GDP, reflecting in part the cancellation of outstanding bilateral debt by Canada, Denmark, France, the former Federal Republic of Germany and the United States. External debt rose modestly to an estimated US$3.1 billion by end 1990, but declined further as a ratio of GDP to 53 per cent.

With the declining repurchase obligations to the Fund and lower levels of commercial debt, the debt service ratio fell from 68 per cent in 1988 to 58 per cent in 1989, and an estimated 40 per cent in 1990.

- Rate of inflation

The average rate of inflation which stood at about 123 per cent in 1983 has varied from about 40 per cent in 1984 to 25 per cent in 1989, rising to 37 per cent in 1990 (Table III). In September 1990, it reached a peak of 41 per cent. This acceleration was partly because of the impact of poor weather on agricultural output; and partly because of the increase in the international price of, and therefore excise taxes on, petroleum. The high levels of excess liquidity in the bank and non-bank public in the first half of 1990 further aggravated the situation. By December 1990, however, it had dropped to 37 per cent, reflecting in part a more forceful and effective implementation of monetary policy.

(d) International macroeconomic situation affecting the external sector

As Ghana's economy is open and highly dependent on commodity exports, especially of cocoa and mineral products, adverse developments in the international economy have invariably had destabilizing effects on the economy.

Recent developments in the world economy and the latest available projections suggest that even though Ghana's average f.o.b. price for cocoa is projected to increase in the medium term, the terms of trade are projected to deteriorate by 4.8 per cent in 1991 following a cumulative loss of 41 per cent during 1987-1990. This is because although export earnings are projected to continue to recover they would still be significantly below (by about 14 per cent) their 1986 levels.

Ghana's most serious concern therefore has been about the uncertainties and slump in commodity prices and the deteriorating terms of trade which have been exacerbated by the suspension of the economic provisions of the International Cocoa Agreement.

Consequently it is expected that better access to markets, particularly for tropical products, and the further strengthening of the GATT-based multilateral trading system by the successful completion of the Uruguay Round would assist Ghana's efforts at diversification away from commodity-based exports and assure it of secure and stable export markets. This explains Ghana's active participation in the Uruguay Round and interest in its successful conclusion.

(iii)   <u>Problems in external markets</u>

Problems faced by Ghana in external markets apart from the instability and plummeting of commodity prices relate to tariffs and non-tariff measures, including tariff escalation, with regard to tropical products.

In the context of the Uruguay Round, therefore, Ghana has submitted indicative lists of tropical products of export interest to her. A copy is attached as Appendix IV.

Appendix I

Balance of Payments, 1984-92
(US$ million)

	1984	1985	1986	1987	1988	1989	Proj. 1990	Proj. 1991	Proj. 1992
Exports (f.o.b.)	567	633	749	824	881	807	826	948	1,051
of which cocoa	382	412	503	495	462	408	355	376	412
Imports (f.o.b.)	-616	-671	-734	-934	-991	-1,000	-1,172	-1,312	-1,355
of which oil*	-161	-210	-123	-141	-143	-156	-215	-250	-221
Trade balance	-49	-39	16	-110	-110	-193	-346	-364	-304
Services net	-229	-254	-291	-316	-327	-312	-334	-364	-382
of which									
interest	-110	-112	-127	-109	-107	-109	-118	-115	-116
Unrequited									
transfers (net)	203	137	190	324	347	422	422	451	448
Current account	-75	-157	-85	-102	-90	-83	-259	-277	-238
Capital account	93	62	20	256	219	200	347	367	328
Official capital (net)	187	32	124	219	188	170	289	344	326
Long-term loans	83	110	227	268	273	286	323	362	368
Inflows	133	135	257	304	308	322	355	391	397
Amortization	-50	-25	-30	-36	-35	-37	-32	-29	-29
Medium-term loans	105	-71	-92	-37	-72	-105	-30	-18	-42
Inflows	170	153	128	109	102	34	63	54	25
Amortization	-65	-223	-220	-146	-174	-138	-93	-72	-67
Trust fund	-1	-7	-11	-12	-13	-11	-4	0	0
Private Capital (net)	-9	6	7	2	4	12	53	19	6
Short-term capital	-85	25	-110	35	27	19	5	5	-4
Errors and omissions	19	-21	8	-15	-4	10	-3	0	0
Overall balance	37	-116	-57	139	125	127	85	90	90
Monetary movements	-37	116	57	-139	-125	-127	-85	-90	-90
of which IMF (net)	214	122	16	-25	-45	4	-48	86	-65
Arrears reduction	-208	-57	-4	-72	-35	-48	-17	0	0

*   Assumes oil prices of US$26.9 per barrel in 1991 and US$22.6 per barrel in 1992.

Source: Minister of Finance and Economic Planning, Bank of Ghana.

Appendix II

GDP by Industrial Origin at Constant 1975 Prices, Growth Rates, 1984-1990
(in percentages)

	1984	1985	1986	1987	1988	1989	1990	1991
Agriculture	9.7	0.6	3.3	0.0	3.6	4.2	-2.4	0.6
Crops & Livestock	15.5	-1.9	0.2	-0.3	6.0	5.1	-4.7	1.8
Cocoa production and marketing	-8.4	13.2	18.2	3.3	-6.3	3.2	3.0	-7.8
Forestry and logging	1.4	0.1	1.2	1.5	3.4	1.2	3.8	4.0
Fishing	0.7	12.0	14.0	-10.1	2.3	0.6	2.3	3.0
Industry	9.1	17.6	7.6	11.5	7.3	4.2	4.4	10.4
Mining & Quarrying	13.5	6.5	-3.0	7.9	17.8	10.0	10.4	38.0
Manufacturing	12.9	24.3	11.0	10.0	5.1	3.0	2.6	7.5
Electricity & water	-6.1	20.7	18.0	18.7	12.9	7.7	9.4	8.8
Construction	2.3	2.8	-2.7	15.9	8.4	4.2	5.2	7.0
Services	6.6	7.5	6.5	9.4	7.8	5.8	8.8	5.2
Transport & communication	12.8	8.5	5.6	10.9	10.2	7.9	12.2	6.0
Wholesale & retail	10.1	13.7	9.0	17.4	7.4	7.5	12.9	6.0
Financial services	9.3	2.6	7.7	5.5	6.7	3.9	7.3	5.5
Government services	0.4	4.6	2.3	3.0	8.2	4.4	4.2	3.5
Other services	9.4	18.3	18.8	19.2	7.6	6.8	9.4	7.0
Less Imputed Charges	7.9	7.8	5.7	9.6	8.9	2.3	2.5	2.8
Plus import duties	20.5	18.8	22.5	0.3	6.0	14.2	7.3	20.0
GDP at market prices	8.6	5.1	5.2	4.8	5.6	5.1	3.1	4.2
Memo item								
Population	3.0	3.3	3.1	3.1	3.0	2.9	3.5	3.0

Source: Minister of Finance and Economic Planning, Bank of Ghana.

Appendix III

Ghana: External Financing Requirements and Resources, 1990-1993
(in millions of US dollars)

	1990 Prog.	1990 Prel.	1991 Prog.	Projections 1992	Projections 1993	Total over 1991-93	Average over 1991-93
Requirements	-827.7	-781.8	-878.3	-659.8	-685.0	-2,223.0	-741.0
Current account deficit, excluding official grants	-489.4	-478.7	-514.0	-466.2	-490.8	-1,471.0	-490.3
Medium- and long-term debt amortization[1]	-103.3	-124.9	-101.4	-96.5	-102.0	-299.9	-100.0
Other capital outflows[2]	-15.7	-7.6	-5.6	-7.0	-2.1	-14.7	-4.9
IMF repurchases[1]	-109.0	-112.6	-80.8	-65.4	-67.6	213.8	-71.3
Trust fund repayments	-3.5	-3.6	-0.5	--	--	-0.5	-0.2
Reduction in payments arrears	-17.3	17.3	--	--	--	--	--
Increase in gross official reserves	-72.7	-20.3	-176.0	-24.6	-22.4	-223.1	-74.4
Reduction in other net foreign[3] liabilities of Bank of Ghana	-16.8	-16.8	--	--	--	--	--
Resources	827.7	781.8	878.3	659.8	685.0	2,223.0	741.0
Official grants (net)	256.6	219.8	236.8	228.0	227.8	692.6	230.9
Long-term loan disbursements	326.3	354.6	390.6	397.0	411.0	1,198.6	399.5
Medium-term loan disbursement	77.9	62.5	54.3	25.3	24.6	104.2	34.7
Other capital inflows	41.0	62.9	29.7	9.5	21.6	60.8	20.3
Bilateral trade agreements	--	17.0	--	--	--	--	--
Use of Fund resources	125.9	166.9	166.9	--	--	166.9	55.6
of which: SAF and ESAF	65.0	--	--	--	--	55.6	--

1 Including short-term capital outflows, and net errors and omissions.
2 Including SAF and ESAF repayments.
3 Excluding external payments arrears and liabilities to the Fund.

Sources: Data provided by the Ghanaian authorities; and Fund and World Bank staff estimates and projections.

Appendix IV

Ghana: Selected Economic and Financial Indicators, 1986-93

	1986	1987	1988	1989	1990 Prog.	1990 Prov.	1991 Prog.	1992 Projections	1993 Projections
					(Annual percentage change, unless otherwise specified)				
National income and prices									
Real GDP	5.2	4.8	5.6	5.1	4.8	2.7	4.0	5.0	5.5
Real GDP per capita	2.5	2.1	2.9	2.4	1.7	0.1	1.4	2.3	2.4
Nominal GDP (in billions of cedis)	511.4	746.0	1,051.2	1,417.2	1,609.1	1,892.1	2,361.4	2,677.8	2,966.3
GDP deflator	41.7	39.2	33.4	28.3	14.0	30.0	20.0	8.0	5.0
Consumer price index (annual average)	24.6	39.8	31.4	25.2	15.0	38.9	23.2	8.0	5.0
Consumer price index (end of period)	33.3	34.2	26.6	30.5	10.0	47.1	10.0	5.0	5.0
External sector									
Exports, f.o.b.	18.5	10.0	6.9	-8.4	-4.4	2.3	14.8	10.9	10.2
Imports, f.o.b.	9.3	27.3	6.1	0.9	8.4	17.2	12.0	3.3	8.6
Export volume	10.8	7.7	11.7	11.2	5.0	7.0	11.1	6.7	4.9
Import volume	13.4	12.8	0.9	1.5	5.1	5.0	3.1	4.4	5.5
Terms of trade	12.5	-8.3	-9.0	-17.2	-11.7	-14.3	-4.8	5.0	2.1
Nominal effective exchange rate	-49.8	-40.4	-17.5	-11.5	...	...	...	...	...
Real effective exchange rate	-42.5	-22.8	-4.1	-6.4	...	...	...	...	...
Government budget [1]									
Revenue and grants	82.6	50.8	38.5	39.5	30.1	24.8	44.1	9.6	8.6
Total expenditure [2]	53.1	45.9	40.1	36.2	25.6	29.5	29.3	9.0	10.8
Current expenditure	58.2	32.5	37.8	33.9	24.7	33.1	29.0	7.9	8.7
Capital expenditure [3]	32.5	111.4	47.2	42.8	28.1	19.8	30.1	12.0	16.9
Money and credit [4] [5]									
Net domestic assets [4] [5]	49.8	11.8	8.5	-10.7	113.0	117.5	4.2	0.9	2.3
Credit to the Government [4] [5]	4.4	-8.6	-7.4	-7.7	103.1	121.3	-17.7	-18.9	-11.2
Credit to the rest of the economy [4] [6]	35.7	14.4	13.3	7.9	13.3	14.6	14.1	17.8	13.4
Broad money	53.7	53.0	43.0	26.9	10.5	17.5	15.0	10.2	10.8
Velocity (GDP/average broad money)	7.6	7.2	7.0	7.0	6.7	7.7	8.2	8.2	8.2
Interest rates (in per cent; end of period)									
Minimum rate on savings deposits	18.5	21.5	17.5	15.0	...	...	...	...	...
Maximum rate on non-agricultural loans	23.0	26.0	30.3	30.5	...	...	...	...	...

(cont'd)

Appendix IV (cont'd)

	1986	1987	1988	1989	1990 Prog.	1990 Prov.	1991 Prog.	1992 Projections	1993 Projections
					(In per cent of GDP)				
Investment and savings									
Gross investment	9.7	13.4	14.2	15.5	17.3	16.0	16.9	18.2	19.5
Gross national savings	10.0	11.2	12.4	13.9	12.4	11.5	12.7	15.0	16.3
Government budget									
Surplus or deficit (-)[2]	0.1	0.5	0.4	0.7	1.4	0.2	1.9	1.9	1.6
Overall surplus or deficit (-)[8]	-3.3	-2.4	-2.7	-2.1	-2.4	-2.4	-1.2	-1.5	-2.2
Revenue and grants	14.4	14.9	14.6	15.1	17.3	14.1	16.3	15.8	15.5
Total expenditure [2]	14.3	14.3	14.3	14.4	15.9	14.0	14.5	13.8	13.9
External sector[7]									
Current account balance[9]	-1.6	-2.3	-1.7	-1.6	-4.9	-4.5	-4.2	-3.2	-3.2
External debt outstanding	51.5	68.3	58.7	55.2	64.3	53.3	53.1	50.8	49.0
Debt service	7.4	11.6	12.7	9.8	7.1	6.3	4.5	3.8	3.5
					(In per cent of exports of goods and services)				
External debt service									
Including the Fund	47.8	58.3	68.0	58.2	38.3	40.0	28.7	24.3	22.6
Excluding the Fund	36.9	31.8	34.0	32.5	21.6	23.3	17.8	16.4	15.7
					(In millions of US dollars)				
Current account balance[9]	-84.8	-101.9	-89.5	-82.8	-232.8	-258.9	-277.1	-238.2	-263.1
Overall balance of payments	-56.7	138.5	124.6	127.4	90.0	85.0	90.0	90.0	90.0
External payments arrears (end of period)	171.4	99.8	65.0	17.3	--	--	--	--	--
Gross international reserves (end of period)	148.7	193.6	200.8	249.0	320.7	269.3	445.3	469.9	492.4
(equivalent weeks of imports c.i.f.)	9.7	9.7	9.6	11.9	13.4	11.0	16.2	16.6	16.0

1 Excluding project-related grants.
2 Excluding capital outlays financed through external project aid.
3 Including net lending and, from 1987 onward, the special efficiency programme.
4 In per cent of broad money at the beginning of the period.
5 The large increase in net domestic assets in 1990 reflects the takeover by the Government of the revaluation losses of the Bank of Ghana.
6 Including financing of the Cocoa Board's operations, but excluding other items (net).
7 Controls on the maximum lending rate and the minimum savings rate were lifted in September 1987 and February 1988 respectively.
8 Including capital expenditure financed through external project aid.
9 Including official grants

Source: Data provided by the Ghanaian authorities; and Fund and World Bank staff estimates and projections.

Appendix V

TROPICAL PRODUCTS

Indicative Lists Submitted by Ghana

The following communication dated 28 September 1988 received from the delegation of Ghana is circulated to all participants.

The Ghana Permanent Mission has the honour to submit Ghana's list of export interest in the area of tropical products.

The Government of Ghana seeks the fullest trade liberalization of tariff and non-tariff measures affecting these products including in their semi-processed and processed forms.

The request lists are addressed to Australia, Austria, Canada, Finland, Japan, New Zealand, Norway, Sweden, Switzerland and United States.

TROPICAL PRODUCTS

Indicative List Addressed by Ghana to Australia

H.S. code	Harmonized commodity description	Tariff rates MFN (current)	GSP	Specific requests TARIFF NTM
0901.11	Coffee: coffee, not roasted; not decaffeinated	2%U	0%	
0901.12	- decaffeinated	2%U	0%	
0901.21	Coffee, roasted - not decaffeinated	2%U	0%	
0901.22	- decaffeinated	2%U	0%	
1801.00	Cocoa beans whole or broken raw or roasted	2%U	0%	
1802.00	Cocoa shells, husks, skins and other waste	2%U	0%	
9403.80	Furniture of cane	30%U	25%	
1203.00	Copra	2%U	0%	
1207.10	Palm nuts and kernels	2%U	0%	
1207.92	Sheanut	2%U	0%	
1511.10	Palm oil and its fractions - crude oil	2%U	0%	
1513.11	Coconut oil and their fractions: - crude oil	2%U (Bounded at ₡0.01 litre and the equivalent of the duty, if any on copra)	0%	
4001.10	Natural Rubber Latex	2%U	0%	
4408	Veneer sheet and sheets for plywood (whether or not sliced) and other wood sawn lengthwise, sliced or peeled, whether or not planed, sanded or finger-jointed, of a thickness not exceeding 6mm:- of the ff: tropical wood - mahogany, obeche etc.	12%B	6%	
4410	Particle of board and similar board of wood or other ligneous materials whether or not agglomerated with resins or other organic binding substances of wood	13%B	6.5%	

(cont'd)

Indicative List Addressed by Ghana to Australia (cont'd)

H.S. code	Harmonized commodity description	Tariff rates MFN (current)	GSP	Specific requests TARIFF NTM
4412.11	Plywood veneered panels and similar laminated wood: plywood consisting solely of sheets of wood, each ply not exceeding 6mm thickness: - with at least one other ply of the ff: tropical wood: mahogany, decks, acejou etc.	18%B	0%	
4412.12	- Other, with at least one outer ply of non-coniferous wood	10%B	0%	
9403.30	Other furniture and parts thereof: - wooden furniture of a kind used in offices	30%U	25%	
9403.50	- wooden furniture of a kind used in the bedroom	30%U	25%	
9403.60	- other wooden furniture	30%U	25%	
9403.90	- parts (of wood)	30%U	25%	

TROPICAL PRODUCTS

Indicative List Addressed by Ghana to Austria

H.S. code	Harmonized commodity description	Tariff rates MFN (current)	GSP	Specific requests TARIFF NTM
0901.11	Coffee, not roasted: not decaffeinated	12%B	0%	
0901.12	- decaffeinated	12%B	0%	
0901.21	- Coffee roasted: - not decaffeinated	15%B 19.5%B	12% 15.6%	
0901.22	- decaffeinated	15%B 19.5%B	12% 15.6%	
1801.00	Cocoa beans, whole or broken, raw or roasted	raw 4%B other 6%B	0%	
1802.00	Cocoa shells husks, skins and other cocoa waste	$1.25/kgU	0%	
1803.20	Whole or partly defatted	15%B	0%	
1804.00	Cocoa butter, fat and oil	5%B	0%	
1805.00	Cocoa powder not containing added sugar or other sweetening matter	27%B	7%	
9403.80	Furniture of cane	8%B	4%	
0804.30	Pineapples; fresh or dried	50.5/kgU	0%	
2009.40	Pineapple Juice	50.80/kg.B 52.70/kg.B	0% 0%	
4408.20	Veneer sheets and sheet for plywood (whether or not sliced) and other wood sawn lengthwise, sliced or peeled, whether or not planed, sanded or finger-jointed of a thickness not exceeding 6mm of mahogany	12%B	6%	
4408.90	Other (not including coniferous)	12%B	6%	

(cont'd)

<u>Indicative List Addressed by Ghana to Austria</u> (cont'd)

H.S. code	Harmonized commodity description	Tariff rates MFN (current)	GSP	Specific requests TARIFF NTM
4412.11	Plywood, veneered panels and similar laminated wood: - plywood consisting solely of sheets of wood, each ply not exceeding 6mm thickness - with at least one outer ply of mahogany	18%B	9%	
4412.12	Other, with at least one outer ply of non-coniferous wood	18%B	9%	
9401.90	Seats and parts thereof: - (parts or wood)	7%B	3.5%	
9403.30	Other furniture and parts thereof: - wooden furniture of a kind used in office	27%B	13.5%	
9403.60	- Other wooden furniture	27%B	13.5%	
9403.90	Parts of wood	23%B	11.5%	

TROPICAL PRODUCTS

Indicative List Addressed by Ghana to Canada

H.S. code	Harmonized commodity description	Tariff rates		Specific requests
		MFN (current)	GSP	TARIFF NTM
0901.21	- Coffee roasted: - not decaffeinated	4.41¢/kgB	0%	
	- decaffeinated	4.41¢/kgB	0%	
1805.00	Cocoa powder not containing added sugar or other sweetening matter	10%B	0%	
9403.80	Furniture of cane	15%P	10%	
1203.00	Palm kernel oil and their fractions: - crude oil	10%B	0%	
1511.10	Palm oil and its fractions - crude oil	10%B	0%	
4407.23	Wood sawn or chipped lengthwise, sliced or peeled whether or not planed, sanded or finger-jointed, of a thickness not exceeding 6mm of other	10%B	4.5%	
4412.11	Plywood, veneered panels and similar laminated wood: - plywood consisting solely of sheets of wood, each ply not exceeding 6mm thickness: with at least one outer ply of mahogany	8%B	5% 6%	
4412.12	- other, with at least one outer ply of non-coniferous wood	8%B	5% 6%	
4401.61	Seats and parts thereof: - parts of wood	1.5%B	10%	
9403.30	Other furniture and parts thereof: - wooden furniture of a kind used in the kitchen	15%B	10%	
9403.60	- Other wooden furniture	15%	0%	
9403.90	- Parts (of wood)	15%	0%	

TROPICAL PRODUCTS

Indicative List Addressed by Ghana to Finland

H.S. code	Harmonized commodity description	Tariff rates (current)		NTM	Specific requests TARIFF NTM
		MFN	GSP		
1207.92	Shea nut	19%	-	Discretionary licence	
1203.00	Copra	19%	-	Discretionary licence	

TROPICAL PRODUCTS

Indicative List Addressed by Ghana to Japan

H.S. code	Harmonized commodity description	Tariff rates MFN (current)	GSP	Specific requests TARIFF NTM
0901.21	Coffee, roasted - - not decaffeinated	20%B	-	
0901.22	Coffee, roast decaffeinated	20%B	-	
1803.10	Cocoa paste, whether or not defatted: - not defatted	10%B	5%	
1803.20	Cocoa wholly or partly defatted	20%B	10%	
1804.00	Cocoa butter, fat and oil	25%B	0%	
1805.00	Cocoa powder not containing added sugar or other sweetening matter	21.5%B	15%	
0904.11	Pepper - neither crushed nor ground	6%B	0%	
0904.12	- Pepper crushed or ground	3.5%B	0%	
0910.10	Ginger	5%B (in retail containers)	0%	
1511.10	Palm oil and its fractions crude oil	7%B	0%	
1513.21	Palm kernel oil and their fractions - crude oil	8%B 720.7/kgB	-	
0804.50	Pineapples fresh or dried	20%U 12%B dried	10% dried	
2009.40	Pineapple Juice	22.5%B not sugared 30%U sugared 35% or ¥27/kgU greater	-	

(cont'd)

Indicative List Addressed by Ghana to Japan (cont'd)

H.S. code	Harmonized commodity description	Tariff rates MFN (current)	GSP	Specific requests TARIFF NTM
4408	Veneer plywood sheets for plywood (whether or not spliced) and other wood sawn lengthwise sliced or peeled, whether or not planed, sanded or finger-jointed, of a thickness not exceeding 6mm: of mahogany	15%P (25%)	0%	
4412.11	Plywood, veneered panels and similar laminated wood: plywood consisting solely of sheets of wood, each ply not exceeding 6mm: thickness of mahogany	8%P	5%	
9403.30	Other furniture and parts thereof: - wooden furniture of a kind used in office	4.8%B 3.8%A	0%	
9403.60	- Other wooden furniture	4%B 3.8%A 4.8%B 3.8%A	0%	
9403.90	- Parts of wood	4.8%B 3.8%A	0%	

TROPICAL PRODUCTS

Indicative List Addressed by Ghana to New Zealand

H.S. code	Harmonized commodity description	Tariff rates MFN (current)	GSP	Specific requests TARIFF NTM
4409	Wood (including strips and friezes for parquet flooring, not assembled continuously shaped (tongued, grooved, rebated, chamfered, V-jointed, beaded, moulded, rounded or the like) along any of its edges or faces whether or not planed sanded or finger-jointed	0%B 10%U	0% 10%	
4410.10	Particle board and similar board of wood or other ligneous materials whether or not agglomerated with resins or other organic binding substances - of wood	20%U	10%	
4412.11	Plywood, veneered panels and similar laminated wood: - plywood consisting solely of sheets of wood, each ply not exceeding 6mm thickness: with at least one other ply of the ff: tropical wood: mahogany, obeche etc	30%U	25%	
4412.12	- Other, with at least one other ply of non-coniferous wood	30%	25%	
9403.30	Other furniture and parts thereof: - wooden furniture of a kind used in offices	34%U	22.5%	
9403.60	- Other wooden furniture	34%U	22.5%	
9403.90	- Parts (of wood)	34%	22.5%	
0901.21	Coffee, roasted - not decaffeinated	25%B	19%	
0901.22	- decaffeinated	25%B	10%	

(cont'd)

Indicative List Addressed by Ghana to New Zealand (cont'd)

H.S. code	Harmonized commodity description	Tariff rates MFN (current)	GSP	Specific requests TARIFF NTM
1803.00	cocoa paste whether or not defatted: not defatted	25.5%B	15%	
1803.20	- wholly or partly defatted	25.5%U	15%	
1805.00	cocoa powder not containing added sugar or other sweetening matter	25.5%U	15%	
9403.80	Furniture of cane	34%U	22.5%	
2306.50	Oil cake and other solid residues: of coconut or copra	10%B 5%	0%	
2306.60	- of palm kernels or nuts	5%	0%	
2009.40	Pineapple juice	5%U	0%	
4407.23	Wood sawn or chipped lengthwise sliced or peeled, whether or not planed, sanded or finger-jointed, of a thickness exceeding 6mm: of mahogany, obeche, etc.	0%B 10%U 30%U	0% 20%	
4408.20	Veneer sheets and sheet for plywood (whether or not sliced) and other wood sawn lengthwise sliced or peeled, whether or not planed sanded or finger-jointed of a thickness not exceeding 6mm: of mahogany, obeche, etc.	10% 25.5%U	0% 20%	

TROPICAL PRODUCTS

Indicative List Addressed by Ghana to Norway

H.S. code	Harmonized commodity description	Tariff rates MFN (current)	GSP	Specific requests TARIFF NTM
0901.21	Coffee, roasted not decaffeinated	NOK 0.50/kg	0%	
0901.22	- decaffeinated	NOK 0.50/kg B	0%	
1803 1804.009 1805.00	- Cocoa paste - Cocoa butter - Cocoa powder not containing added sugar or other sweetening matter	NOK 0.40/kgB	0%	
9403.80	Furniture (Cane)	4.2%B	0%	
1203.00	Coconut oil and its fractions - crude oil	NOK 0.16/kgU	0%	
1513.21	Palm kernel oil and their fractions - crude oil	NOK 0.16/kgU	-	
2009.40	Pineapple juice	0% (in containers weighing, with contents, 3kg or more, not containing added sugar or other sweetening matter. NOK 0.50/kgB	0%	

TROPICAL PRODUCTS

Indicative List Addressed by Ghana to Sweden

H.S. code	Harmonized commodity description	Tariff rates MFN (current)	GSP	NTN	Specific requests TARIFF NTM
1203.00	Copra	Variable levy	-	Special fee	
1207.92	Shea nut	Variable levy	-	Special fee	

TROPICAL PRODUCTS

Indicative List Addressed by Ghana to Switzerland

H.S. code	Harmonized commodity description	Tariff rates MFN (current)	GSP	Specific requests TARIFF NTM
0901.11	Coffee: coffee not roasted: not decaffeinated	SWF 0.50/ kg.B	-	
0901.21	Coffee, roasted: - not decaffeinated	SWF 0.90/ kg.B	SWF 6.63/ kg	
0901.22	Coffee decaffeinated	SWF 0.90/	SWF 0.63/ kg	
1802.00	Cocoa husks, shells, skins and other cocoa waste	SWF 0.01/ kgU	-	
1803.10	Cocoa paste whether or not defatted: not defatted	SWF 0.40/ kg.B	0%	
1804.00	Cocoa butter fat and oil	SWF 0.025/ kg.B	0%	
1805.00	Cocoa powder not containing added sugar or other sweetening matter	SWF 0.28/ kgB	SWF 0.24/ kg	
0904.11	Pepper - neither crushed nor ground	0%	-	
0910.10	Ginger crushed or ground	SWF 0.15/ kg.B	0%	
1203.00	Copra	SWF 0.001/ kgU	-	
1207.10	Palm nuts and kernels	SWF 0.001/ kg.U	-	
1207.92	Sheanut	SWF 0.001/ kgU	-	
1511.10	Palm oil and its fractions - crude oil (not for human consumption)	SWF 0.001/ kgP	0%	

(cont'd)

Indicative List Addressed by Ghana to Switzerland (cont'd)

H.S. code	Harmonized commodity description	Tariff rates MFN (current)	GSP	Specific requests TARIFF NTM
1513.21	Palm kernel oil and their fractions - crude oil	SWF 0.1/kgP	0%	
2305.00	Oil cake and other solid residue: of copra	SWF 0.002/kgU	0%	
2306.60	- of palm nuts or kernels	SWF 0.002/kgU	0%	
0804.30	Pineapples fresh or dried	SWF 0.15/ kgB	SWF 0.11/ kg	
2009.40	Pineapple Juice	SWF 0.25/kgB SWF 0.70/kgB	SWF 0.52/ kg	

TROPICAL PRODUCTS

Indicative List Addressed by Ghana to United States

H.S. code	Harmonized commodity description	Tariff rates MFN (current)	GSP	Specific requests TARIFF NTM
0804.30	Pineapples, Fresh or Dried	0.64¢/ kg.B	-	
2009.40	Pineapple Juice	5.3¢/ kg.B	-	
1803.20	Cocoa - wholly or partly defatted	0.82¢/ kg.B	0%	
1805.00	Cocoa powder not containing added sugar or other sweetening matter	0.82¢/ kg.B	0%	
0904.11	Pepper - neither crushed nor ground	0%	-	
0910.10	Ginger crushed or ground	0%B 2.2¢/ kg.B	0%	
9403.80	Furniture of cane bamboo	9.7%B	0%	
1203.00	Copra	4.1¢/ kg.B		
1511.10	Palm oil and its fractions - crude oil	1.1¢/ kg.B	-	
2306.00	Oil cake and other solid residue of coconut or copra	0.7%¢/ kg.U	0%	
2303.60	Oil cake and other solid residue of palm nuts or kernels	0.7¢/ kg.U	0%	
4412	Plywood, veneered panels and similar laminated wood: plywood consisting solely of sheets of wood each ply not exceeding 6mm thickness with at least one outer ply of the ff. tropical woods: mahogany etc.	8%B	-	
9403.40	Seats and parts thereof: - parts of wood	6.6%B 5.3%B	0%	
9403.30	Other furniture and parts thereof - wooden furniture of a kind used in office	6.6%B 2.5%B	0%	
9403.90	Other furniture parts thereof - parts of wood	5.3%B	0%	

PART C

MINUTES OF THE COUNCIL MEETING

CONTENTS

The concluding remarks by the Chairman of the Council are published in Part A.

I.   <u>INTRODUCTORY REMARKS BY THE CHAIRMAN OF THE COUNCIL</u>

The Chairman, introducing the Trade Policy Review of Ghana, noted that this would be based on reports prepared by the Government of Ghana (document C/RM/G/21) and the Secretariat (documents C/RM/S/21A and 21B). The Government report had followed the agreed outline format (L/6552). The Secretariat had sought clarification from the Government on factual information contained in its report. The procedures for the meeting were set out in document C/RM/9.

Participants were invited to adopt two main themes during the review. Ghana's general objectives of trade policies, including approaches to trade liberalization, should be followed by a discussion of the major trade policy instruments used for achieving its industrial policy objectives, including sectoral plans.

He invited the representative of Ghana to make his introductory remarks, to be followed by the two discussants, Mr. Andras Szepesi and Mr. Somchin Suntavaruk.

II.   REMARKS BY THE REPRESENTATIVE OF GHANA

Ghana welcomes the opportunity to discuss its trade policies and practices under the Trade Policy Review Mechanism. In view of the extensive documentation contained in both the Government and Secretariat reports, our introductory statement will concentrate on major developments in trade liberalization since these reports were prepared.

As contracting parties may be aware, Ghana has been carrying out a comprehensive programme of financial, trade and structural reforms since 1983 aimed at improving resource allocation within the economy and enhancing the efficiency of production, both for the domestic and external markets.

The key elements of these reforms have been the:

(a)   re-alignment of relative prices to encourage productive activities, promote exports and strengthen economic incentives;

(b)   progressive shift away from direct controls and intervention towards greater reliance on market forces;

(c)   restoration of fiscal and monetary discipline;

(d)   rehabilitation of economic and social infrastructure;   and

(e)   reduction of state involvement in direct production and the enhancement of the rôle of the private sector in all spheres of the economy.

In the trade and payments area there has been a consistent policy of eliminating all forms of controls. A major aspect of the liberalization programme was the introduction in September 1986 of the Foreign Exchange Auction system under which the exchange rate of the Cedi is market determined in the context of weekly auctions. As part of the continuing liberalization process of the trade and payments system, the Government has, since March 1988, authorized the establishment of Forex Bureaux where the public can freely purchase or sell foreign exchange at open market prices.

In January 1989, the import licensing system which, since the early 1960s had been the main instrument applied by Ghana to regulate imports, was abolished.

A key area of the trade regime which has also seen further liberalized is tariff administration. The thrust has been towards a lower and more uniform tariff structure. This has involved a lowering of the average tariff rate from 50 per cent in 1983 to the current low level of about 20 per cent.

Since the reports were published, we have taken further measures to rationalize our tariff and tax structures, and to increase private sector incentives. The super sales tax imposed on luxury goods in the 1990 fiscal year, and which initially ranged from 75 to 500 per cent before being lowered to a range of 10 to 100 per cent during the 1991 fiscal year, was completely abolished from January 1992. Additionally, the special tax on some imports which ranged from 10 to 40 per cent has been rationalized and reduced to a maximum rate of 10 per cent. There has also been a scaling down of import and sales taxes on motor cars. Import duties and sales tax on all building materials have been abolished.

A current preoccupation of the Ghanaian Government is to find ways of making the private sector the real engine of growth, while the public sector focuses on the effective implementation of policy reforms to increase competition; better manage trimmer public enterprises; and on improving physical and social infrastructure - education, training, science and technology to create and sustain an enabling environment for long-term development.

Towards that end, and to stimulate increased investment in the private sector, a number of measures have been taken to enhance after-tax rates of return:

(a)   the corporate tax rate for commerce, printing and publishing has been reduced from 50 per cent to the standard rate of 35 per cent applicable to agriculture, manufacturing and the construction sectors;

(b)   the corporate tax rate for the financial sector has been reduced from 50 to 45 per cent to encourage banks to reduce lending rates; and

(c)   the dividend withholding tax has been reduced from 15 to 10 per cent.

The Government is also carrying out a thorough review of the legal and regulatory framework, as well as the tax and financial regimes which govern the private sector, with the view to making appropriate changes to enhance the growth of the private sector.

As is widely acknowledged, we have since 1983 succeeded in transforming our economy from an inward-looking one to an outward-oriented economy ready to participate fully in the multilateral trading system.

This outward orientation, however, increases our vulnerability to adverse trends in the international economic system, in particular, to possible slumps in world commodity prices and deteriorating terms of trade. Consequently, better access to markets, especially for tropical products and the further strengthening of the GATT-based multilateral trading system through the successful completion of the Uruguay Round, would assist Ghana's efforts at diversification away from commodity-based exports, and provide secure and stable export markets. Hence, Ghana's active participation in the Uruguay Round and interest in its successful conclusion.

III. GENERAL OBJECTIVES OF TRADE POLICIES

(1) Statement by the first discussant

The first discussant noted that, although only one standard should apply to all trade policy reviews, certain features of the Ghanaian economy are worth bearing in mind. Ghana was a low-income developing country, with GDP per capita of some US$400 and heavy export dependence on cocoa. Moreover, the radical change in direction of Ghana's trade policies since launching its Economic Recovery Programme in 1983, needed to be assessed against its previous inward-looking trade policies of promoting import-substitution industries which, together with general economic mismanagement, had precipitated the severe economic crisis of the 1960s and 1970s.

Since trade and exchange liberalization were the centrepiece of Ghana's economic reforms, it would be interesting for the Council to examine Ghana's experience with past protectionist policies. What were the main factors behind Ghana's shift towards import-opening measures, the rationale for the chosen sequencing of trade and economic reforms, and the factors determining the pace and priority attached to individual reform elements? How successful had been its transition to a more open economy?

While Ghana's trade policies no doubt still suffered from a number of imperfections and inconsistencies, the post-1983 unilateral trade policy reforms appeared to have been successful from a broader GATT perspective. Progressive liberalization, including the introduction of a market-based exchange regime and abolition of the comprehensive import licensing system in 1989 when Article XVIII:B was revoked, as well as tariff reductions implemented in four stages, had facilitated structural change and enhanced economic efficiency by exposing domestic industries to greater international competition.

Although much remains to be done, tribute was to be paid to the substantial progress in Ghana's trade and economic reforms. These had contributed to a smoother functioning of the multilateral trading system, through increased compliance by Ghana to the underlying disciplines embodied in the General Agreement. He wondered to what extent Ghana's development and reform programmes had been affected by the trade policies of individual contracting parties, as well as collective actions exercised within GATT.

A related point concerned the expected impact on the economy, and on the future direction of reforms in Ghana, of a successful conclusion to the Uruguay Round. To what extent are Ghana's future reforms likely to be affected by the Uruguay Round outcome, including improved market access for tropical products?

Finally, a critical rôle was played in economic reforms by external assistance agencies, such as the multilateral institutions like the World Bank and the IMF, as well as country donors. How important had the provision of such assistance been to the reform process, and what forms of assistance had been most useful?

(2) <u>Statement by the second discussant</u>

The second discussant referred to the poor economic performance which led to the turnaround in trade and economic policies since 1983, as well as Ghana's continued vulnerability through its high export and import dependency. Traditional primary products, namely tropical products, especially cocoa, forestry, fishing and mining, such as gold, diamonds, manganese and bauxite, continued to dominate exports, despite some limited growth in non-traditional products. Ghana's export dependency was now matched under the reform programme by a growing dependency on imported inputs, such as fuels, chemicals and machinery.

In the face of these structural constraints, Ghana had courageously embarked on a programme of gradually reforming and fine-tuning its trade policies to achieve its objectives of an adequate supply of industrial raw materials; improved international competitiveness of agricultural products; and export growth and diversification. An important precondition was the increased rôle of the private sector in business activities and trade policy formulation, such as through holding high level meetings with government officials. He asked what was seen as the appropriate balance between the Government's rôle and that of the private sector? Furthermore, although some State-owned enterprises were being privatized, many parastatals continued to operate, albeit in competition with private firms. It remained to be seen how their future import policies would contribute to opening Ghana's market.

Another fundamental feature of Ghana's reforms was the movement from the dual exchange rate system, an inefficient allocator of resources, towards a single rate. Ghana's reforms had greatly enhanced its capacity to participate in the multilateral system and to share in the benefits of improved and strengthened trade rules and disciplines that would result from a successful Uruguay Round. It remained to be seen how, and in what way, Ghana's reform programme would be affected by the outcome of the Uruguay Round.

(3) <u>Statements and questions by members of the Council</u>

The representative of <u>Canada</u> sought additional details and clarification on the impending National Tax Tribunal and its rôle in Customs matters; the likely content and timing of the redrafted trade laws; progress on the Government's privatization programme; and the consultant's report on areas affecting trade policy, such as structural adjustment, export diversification, industry protection and greater domestic value added in natural resource-based products. Ghana's views were also requested on its involvement in regional initiatives, such as the proposed African Economic Community, and ECOWAS. Particular information was sought concerning the impact of restricting ECOWAS benefits to firms with community status.

The representative of the European Communities welcomed Ghana's trade reforms as consistent with the Communities' general support for policies aimed at avoiding fluctuations in effective protection, such as the elimination of non-tariff barriers and the implementation of more uniform tariff regimes. The Lomé Convention provided Ghana duty-free access to its major trading partner, EC markets, for all goods, except certain agricultural products. This preferential treatment would not be affected by the single EC market. Certain trade promotion programmes existing under the Convention could also help Ghana diversify its exports. Based on the EC's experience, Ghana was encouraged to pursue regional initiatives towards integration as an indispensable step in the country's development.

The representative of the United States recalled the challenges to the world trading system of creating an external environment that would support Ghana's substantial trade and structural reforms, and help keep them on track. She indicated that access to foreign exchange still appeared to be the major obstacle restricting imported inputs. Details were sought on Ghana's plans to bind tariffs within the Uruguay Round and its redrafted patent legislation.

The representative of Brazil appreciated the significant autonomous trade liberalization undertaken in Ghana, given its economic difficulties. Additional trade reforms would further improve transparency and resource allocation. Trading partners had an important responsibility to support Ghana's reforms by reducing tariffs and eliminating other trade barriers, thereby opening their markets to Ghanaian exports. In view of the export sector's importance to Ghana's development, export incentives should be recognized as valid trade policy instruments for promoting domestic value added in natural resource-based products, provided such measures did not impose excessive strains on the domestic economy.

The representative of Sweden, speaking also on behalf of Iceland, Finland and Norway, welcomed Ghana's trade reforms. He mentioned some minor remaining obstacles restricting imports, such as the slowness in refunding duties under the drawback scheme for exporters. Ghana, like other developing countries, should increase the predictability of the trading system and reduce uncertainty amongst producers and traders by binding its tariffs, as well as lowering rates. Furthermore, Ghana's contribution to the GATT system would be enhanced by signing MTN agreements. Details were sought on the comprehensive trade law currently being redrafted, as well as Ghana's views on the functioning and future rôle of ECOWAS.

The representative of <u>Japan</u> appreciated the substantial market-opening measures that had contributed to Ghana's economic expansion. However, he noted that a number of measures in Ghana's trading system, including tariffs, temporarily protected domestic industries to counter economic difficulties, such as falling world cocoa prices and deteriorating terms of trade.

The representative of <u>Switzerland</u> commented on the positive economic results experienced in Ghana following trade liberalization. These included exchange and foreign investment reforms. He also welcomed the progress achieved in democratization. Greater transparency was, however, needed in Ghana's taxation and tariff structures, including the numerous concessional tariff arrangements.

The representative of <u>Egypt</u> raised the importance of export diversification in reducing Ghana's vulnerability to fluctuations in world commodity prices, and attracting increased foreign investment in all sectors. Ghana was urged to attach additional priority to trading with other developing countries.

The representative of <u>Tanzania</u> noted the limited export diversification so far achieved by Ghana and sought details on external constraints confronted by Ghana in attempting to broaden its export base.

The representative of <u>Australia</u> raised the absence of tariff bindings by Ghana. This substantially diminished tariff predictability and created uncertainty for producers and traders. He wondered whether Ghana would consider binding tariffs under the Uruguay Round. He noted the importance to Ghana's reform process of achieving a successful conclusion to the Uruguay Round and improving market access in areas, like tropical products and agriculture, vital for its export diversification and growth. Other matters raised by the Australian representative included the promotion of private investment and exports as well as the intended acceleration of Ghana's ongoing privatization programme, especially for larger mining enterprises.

IV.   USE OF MAJOR TRADE POLICY INSTRUMENTS

(1)   Statement by the first discussant

The first discussant stated that traditional import substitution policies for Ghana were inappropriate, since improved export performance required access to imported inputs. Trade reforms, such as several tariff changes, including in special import taxes - the major import barrier following the elimination of quantitative restrictions - have been an important factor behind recent import growth. Apart from unbound tariffs, minimum import prices were implemented in conjunction with Ghana's pre-shipment inspection system.

Export incentives, especially the income tax rebate, had assisted export diversification and growth. However, the generous financial benefits offered to major exporters through lower income tax payments could reduce domestic supplies by diverting funds to exports. Other measures directed at improving export performance included investment incentives, duty-free imports for exporters, and Government expenditure on export promotion.

(2)   Statement by the second discussant

The second discussant referred to the importance of promoting a broader export base for Ghana. The country continued to be highly dependent on cocoa, despite some minor diversification towards non-traditional food exports. Although import liberalization had in part encouraged this process, exports were assisted by, for example, the income tax rebate scheme. An important issue for discussion was whether the provision of export assistance could contradict the objective of improving economic efficiency.

Similarly, the efficacy might be questioned of using export restrictions to promote domestic processing of natural resource-based products, such as timber products, as a means of generating employment and achieving environmental goals. Increased use of these measures by Ghana could adversely affect trading partners.

Although self-sufficiency was no longer a stated policy objective, the Government clearly saw agricultural development as a vital engine for sustained economic growth. How was this growth to be generated, and what would be the rôle of Government in this area?

(3)   Statements and questions by members of the Council

The representative of the United States, in response to introductory comments made by the Chairman that the Council limit its discussion to existing GATT arrangements covering merchandise trade, pointed out her understanding that the Mechanism was intended to review all aspects of a contracting parties' trade-related policies. Previous reviews had already examined areas such as investment, services trade and competition policies.

Ghana had a good record in protecting intellectual property rights. It was a member of both the World Intellectual Property Organization and the African Intellectual Property Organization. Since Independence, prior registration of patents had been required in the United Kingdom. However, its patent legislation was currently being redrafted. She requested details on any likely changes. Questions were also raised on the need for additional export and investment incentives; Ghana's views on binding tariffs within the Uruguay Round; and the rationale for setting minimum export prices.

The representative of Canada questioned the negative effects on investment and efficiency of the relatively high protection afforded to domestic industries by the existing four-tiered tariff structure, and the absence of tariff bindings. The increasing use of export prohibitions in the forest products sector and their debilitating impact on the competitiveness of industries relying on these measures was also raised. Finally, reference was made to the non-transparent and arbitrary nature of Ghana's anti-dumping procedures and the remedy of applying special import taxes at the tariff line level. Ghana was asked whether it would consider joining the Anti-dumping Code, as well as other MTN Codes in which it had observer status.

The representative of Australia referred to the tendency for tariff disparities to widen, leading to increased effective protection, due largely to higher duties and special taxes on imports of consumer goods as well as concessional arrangements, such as end-use tariff concessions. He wondered whether a more uniform assistance structure would further improve economic performance, by inducing more efficient resource allocation and diversification of Ghana's production and export base. Details were sought on any proposed trade reforms.

V.   RESPONSE BY THE REPRESENTATIVE OF GHANA

In responding to the matters raised by Council (see Sections III and IV), the representative of Ghana stated that trade policy reforms implemented since 1983 must be seen in the context of Ghana's overall development and past experiences. The Government now clearly recognized the failure of previous import-substitution policies, and that it was important to further liberalize trade under the recovery programme. It remained committed to systematically and gradually achieving lower, more uniform tariff rates. In this regard, the 1992-94 programme provided for, to the extent permitted by budgetary requirements, reduced tariff rates, abolition of special import taxes and lower coverage of duty exemptions and concessions.

Export diversification and promotion to reduce Ghana's vulnerability to world commodity price fluctuations was seen as an important aspect of the Government's reform strategies. This included further reducing overdependency on cocoa and encouraging the growth of non-traditional manufactured products, such as fish, salt, aluminium and wood products. Some success has been achieved in this area. Exports were expected to continue growing from US$62 million currently to some US$300 million by 1995.

The activities of the Ghana Export Promotion Council in providing marketing and other assistance, especially for selected areas thought to offer greatest potential - including agricultural commodities like pineapples, ginger and black pepper, as well as manufactured wooden furniture, aluminium products, processed foods, soaps, detergents and traditional-type textiles like batik - had been important in this regard. It was emphasized that the minimum export prices set by the Promotion Council were only indicative for use as a guide by exporters in their commercial transactions, and did not prevent lower prices from being negotiated by the exporter to reflect prevailing market conditions.

The Government, as part of its policies for expanding the rôle played by the private sector, was committed to the privatization programme. A number of State-owned enterprises had, or were in the process of being, divested; all three of the mines formerly owned by the State Gold Mining Enterprise were being sold, and part-sale was being offered of the main mine of the Ghana Consolidated Diamond Company. The Government had also undertaken a number of measures to promote private sector involvement, such as tax reforms, restructuring of the financial system and establishment of a stock exchange.

Most state-owned enterprises were not statutory monopolies, with the notable exception of the marketing activities of the Ghana Cocoa Board (COCOBOD). Its monopoly position over coffee and sheanuts ended recently, however, by allowing private operators to market these products. Similar steps were to be taken in 1992 to enable domestic cocoa sales to be traded privately, while at the same time retaining the Board's monopoly controls over cocoa exports and quality certification.

Ghana's trade reforms were supported by overseas remittances of around US$200 million annually and by financial assistance from both multilateral and bilateral sources. External funds had augmented Ghana's foreign exchange levels, moderating Ghana's balance of payments problems and assisting in the rehabilitation of physical and social infrastructure necessary for Ghana's economic development.

The Government's view was that further tariff reductions should precede any binding commitments by Ghana. However, the Government accepted that tariff bindings at ceiling rates above existing levels might increase predictability in the trading environment, and was prepared therefore to consider this issue seriously.

The planned Tax Tribunal, to be established under legislation already passed, would have High Court jurisdiction over all matters relating to customs duties and taxes. Aggrieved parties would in future be able to seek redress from the Tribunal against Customs decisions, and rulings by the Tribunal will be appealable through the Courts.

Many laws, such as the Exchange Control Act, the Manufacturing Industry Act and the basic trade legislation, were currently being reviewed to bring them into line with existing policies. The redrafted trade law would reinforce the thrust of recent reforms and enforce the interests of multilateral trade. Ghana was considering joining the MTN agreements on Technical Barriers to Trade, Customs Valuation, Government Procurement and Import Licensing. Accession to MTN agreements would, however, depend on the outcome of the Uruguay Round.

Given the sector's predominance in the Ghanaian economy, agricultural development occupied a central rôle of the Government's strategy for economic growth. Policies have shifted away from direct Government involvement in agricultural production to providing necessary marketing services and infrastructure, such as storage and limited irrigation facilities, for private sector development.

Following world wide trends, regional initiatives were receiving renewed interest in Ghana as a means of facilitating the country's export growth and diversification. This was reflected in the recent changes in the trade liberalization scheme undertaken by ECOWAS members, and the longer term plan to consolidate regional trading groups into the proposed African Economic Community. The objective of these regional arrangements was to reinforce multilateral trade. Ghana was also hopeful that its goals of export diversification and growth would be aided by a successful conclusion to the Uruguay Round, through improved market access for

Ghanaian exports, especially for tropical and natural resource-based products.

VI.   OTHER STATEMENTS

The <u>first discussant</u> referred to views expressed by participants that external support and encouragement was important to keep Ghana's reform efforts on track and to make them even more consistent with GATT ideals. In this regard, a clear consensus had emerged from the review that an early and successful conclusion to the Uruguay Round would, through aiding stability, predictability and improving market access for Ghanaian exports, make an essential contribution to the continued success of Ghana's trade and economic reforms.

The <u>second discussant</u> stated that in promoting open-market policies, like those implemented in Ghana which no doubt contributed to improved economic performance, difficulties often arose in conforming with the multilateral rules and disciplines; meeting conflicting domestic interests; satisfying plurilateral international relationships; and reflecting important non-trade concerns.

The representative of <u>Madagascar</u> referred to Ghana's tremendous achievements as a developing country in setting up a market-based economy and contributing to the multilateral trading system.

The representative of the <u>European Communities</u> raised several matters, such as Ghana's desire to achieve improved market access for tropical and natural resource-based products under the Uruguay Round as a means of achieving export diversification and growth.